Emotional Confidence

BY THE SAME AUTHOR:

Anger Control Workout (Thorsons Audio)
Assert Yourself
Confident Children
Emotional Confidence (Thorsons Audio)
Managing Anger
The Positive Woman
Self-esteem
Self-motivation
Self-motivation (Thorsons Audio)
Super Confidence

Emotional Confidence

Gael Lindenfield
Illustrations by Jessica Stockham

Thorsons
An Imprint of HarperCollins*Publishers*

Thorsons
An Imprint of HarperCollins*Publishers*
77–85 Fulham Palace Road,
Hammersmith, London W6 8JB
1160 Battery Street,
San Francisco, California 94111-1213

Published by Thorsons 1997
5 7 9 10 8 6 4

Gael Lindenfield asserts the moral right to
be identified as the author of this work

A catalogue record for this book
is available from the British Library

ISBN 0 7225 3245 8

Printed and bound in Great Britain by
Caledonian International Book Manufacturing Ltd, Glasgow

To Katherine Edwards

– to whom I shall be everlastingly grateful for underpinning my own emotional confidence with so much practical and emotional support during those testing few weeks following the death of my daughter Laura

Contents

Acknowledgements

I would like to thank *everyone* who has given me and my family emotional and practical help during these very difficult last 18 months. Without your support this book could certainly not have been written.

I am particularly grateful to my editor, Wanda Whiteley, and many other staff at Thorsons who always responded with such care and concern when I informed them of yet another setback in the writing of this book. I know that the late delivery of the manuscript has caused pressure to very many people who have been involved in its production and I am so appreciative of their willingness to work at breakneck speed to enable us to reach our deadline date.

I would also like to thank Tiffany Thomas for helping me with the background academic research to the book.

Finally, I would like to thank my husband Stuart, for his unfailing emotional support and for getting up at the crack of dawn to do yet another edit on yet another book.

Introduction

Do you really practise what you preach?
The theory's fine but have you tried it out in real life?
Everyday problems – yes, but would you and your strategies
stand the test of a major trauma?

Challenging but highly justified questions which have been
thrown at me throughout my career, not just by interested or
cynical others but by my own carping conscience. When writing a book, in particular, I have had to learn to live with this
kind of unrelenting internal inquisition. But never until I took
on the task of this one has 'real life' put me and my manuscript
through so many continual testing trials.

For many years I had been wanting to write a self-help programme to help others develop the emotional skills which I
had to acquire for myself in such a random 'pot-luck' fashion
over several decades. For most of my early adult life my
'uncontrollable' feelings had wrought havoc on my life and
health. Learning how to take control of the emotional side of
me had been a crucial factor in the building of my own self-
confidence, had enabled me to be the kind of person I could
respect and had given me the kind of lifestyle and relationships
I had always wanted.

I was therefore thrilled when, in January 1996 at a brainstorming session with my editor, I finally settled on the title
and plan for this book. I returned from London inspired and

motivated. My brain was buzzing with exciting ideas for new strategies and exercises. A few days later, on the morning of Sunday, January 28th, I sat with my diary and began to outline my writing schedule. By 9 o'clock that same evening, however, my own emotional confidence had completely collapsed: my 19-year-old daughter Laura had been killed in a freak car accident and I was living my most dreaded nightmare.

I plunged hysterically into an uncontrollable whirlpool of intense grief and deep despair. Not only did I think I would never again recover my emotional equilibrium, I didn't actually *want* to do so. When the following day I began to be taunted by an inner voice which said, *'Now, let's see if your fancy theories can get you through this one, then!'*, I found I didn't care. My whole life, not just my work, seemed pointless. I no longer felt the person I thought I was. I rejected comfort and was useless at comforting. I was quite unable to help even those whom I loved and who shared my pain.

But my inner voice was wrong. Today, 18 months later, not only has my emotional health been repaired, I am convinced that it has also been strengthened. Furthermore, I have written this book in spite of a number of other serious setbacks during the last year.

So it is with increased confidence in its contents that I am writing this Introduction. I am quite sure that without the knowledge and skills which I am now sharing I would not have had the strength or motivation to take up my life again in the way that I know Laura would have wanted me to do.

What Is Emotional Confidence?

This is a short-hand term which I use to describe a particular component of self-confidence. We sense it within ourselves when we know we can rely on our ability to be in full control of our feelings.

When I am working on changing some aspect of myself or my behaviour, I have always found it helpful to keep an image of an ideal role-model in my mind. Although 'good-enough' standards are all that are required, this imaginary, faultless figure is an inspirational and a useful measuring tool.

Portrait of a Paragon

Should some fortunate person ever possess rock-solid, enduring emotional confidence, we would expect them to be able to:

- freely experience a full rich range of emotions from deep despair and gut anger to exhilarating joy and tender love without ever worrying that their heart will rule their head – so they would never think or say:
  'I don't know what's happened to me, I just feel dead inside'
  'Nothing seems to get me excited anymore'
  'I've lost my sense of fun'
  'I never get angry – what's the point?'
  'I haven't cried for years'
- be fully aware of what they are feeling at the time they are experiencing an emotion
  – so they would never think or say:
  'I don't know what I feel'
  'When I left there I realized just how angry I was, I only wish that I had said ...'
  'It wasn't until she started flirting with someone else that I realized I really loved her'
  'I'd been so busy that I hadn't noticed how lonely I was beginning to feel'
- keep their emotional responses under their own control
  – so they would never think or say:
  'I loved him/her too much – I couldn't stop myself from ...'
  'I just flipped – I don't know what came over me'
  'I suddenly found myself being as jealous/envious as hell, so I couldn't resist ...'
  'I started to blush and sweat – I had to leave'
  'The tears just came – I couldn't hold them back'
- readily and steadily fire themselves up with motivational feeling

– so they would never think or say:

'I set goals, but then I just seem to lose interest'

'I want to change, I'm just too lazy to make the effort'

'I just don't care enough anymore – even though I know I ought to'

'I've lost heart'

- express their feelings at the 'right' time and in the 'right' place, and to the 'right' person

  – so they would never think or say:

  'I started to shake and I couldn't stop – it was so embarrassing'

  'I really love her, but I always seem to choose the wrong moment to show it'

  'We were driving into work and I just flew at him – he had to slam on the brakes'

  'I was so mad at him that, when I got home, I just snapped at everyone'

- respond sensitively and sensibly to the emotional states of other people

  – so they would never think or say:

  'I always seem to put my big foot in it, and embarrass everyone'

  'I just didn't notice how anxious he was – if I had, I'd have stopped pressurizing him'

  'I didn't realize she was in such a bad mood – I ought to have known because ...'

  'He looked so disappointed, I couldn't resist – I was stupid because ...'

  'She was so angry, I just clammed up even though ...'

Unless after reading this you have discovered yourself to be the only paragon of emotional confidence on earth, this book was written for you!

How to Use This Book

I have designed this self-help programme so that you can work on it over a set period of time, either on your own or in a small group. Reading it and completing the exercises will, first, give you more understanding of how your emotions work, and secondly improve your ability to manage specific feelings. I am hoping that after using it in this way you will continue to keep it in a handy position, because I have tried to design it in such a way that it can be a useful practical tool. Should you ever experience a problem with a feeling in the future (and who won't?!), you will be able to dip into the relevant section, take some support and remind yourself of a strategy which will help you to regain your control.

A Quick Tour through the Book

Why We Need Emotional Confidence

This section is designed to boost your motivation, so I have listed 25 reasons for building and maintaining emotional confidence. I hope that these will inspire you not just to skim lightly through the rest of the book but to work mentally as you read!

Part 1: Three Keys to Building Emotional Confidence

Key 1: Tame Your Temperament
– with emotional understanding and skill

In **Understanding How Feelings Work** I have given a brief explanation of how our emotional responses function, and a simple summary of research findings we have to date. There are exercises and check-lists which will help you apply this theory to your own everyday experience of your feelings.

In **Skills for Taking Control** you will find a questionnaire designed to help you assess the level of your current emotional skills. Should you find that these need improving, I have also given you some suggestions and examples of a few of my own favourite techniques.

Key 2: Soothe Your Sensitivity
– with effective emotional healing

In this section you will find a fully illustrated explanation of my Emotional Healing Strategy for dealing effectively with feelings such as sadness, hurt and disappointment. I explain this strategy in depth, with appropriate exercises.

Key 3: Harness Your Habits
– with positive strategies for runaway feelings

In this section you will find tips, strategies and exercises to help you take control of your self-sabotaging emotional habits. It first introduces a general Quick-Fix strategy called ACHE; then the focus shifts to eight specific emotions which many people find difficult to control at times. These are:

Guilt	Fear
Shame	Jealousy
Envy	Apathy
Anger	Unbridled Love

Even if these are not the emotions you tend to find difficult, you should be able to use the approaches and exercises offered to work on the ones with which you do have difficulty.

Part 2

This includes some suggestions for maintaining emotional confidence and helping to foster it in others. It also includes the Further Reading and Resources chapter, the Index and some blank pages for your own notes.

To Read On or Not to Read On – Is that Your Question?

You have probably gathered by now that this book is not necessarily going to be a quick or easy read. You may even have glanced through its pages and begun to feel a little daunted. This is an understandable reaction and one which is very familiar to me. In fact, whenever I am faced with changing any aspect of my feelings or behaviour, I feel this way. I then find myself automatically thinking of a million and one reasons why I don't need or want to take up the challenge, now or ever. I start to put up a convincing case for not having the time or the energy to devote to the work, or I don my cynic's hat and focus on the other problems this work won't solve, or I persuade myself that I haven't the difficulty after all!

In my case, this self-sabotaging thinking process is merely a pre-programmed response to uncomfortable feelings (usually of fear and anxiety). I have learned to take some 'time out' – to calm down and take control of my feelings before making my decision. This usually involves doing a familiar activity which both relaxes and reassures me (e.g. a warm aromatic bath or a good clear-up in the kitchen accompanied by my favourite music.). I find I am then more willing and able to look at the challenge in a more rational way.

So, before making your decision to read on, why not give yourself a nurturing and encouraging treat? Once you have done that, set aside some time to dip in and out of this book for a while. Read the Contents page and mark the bits which are a priority for *you*. Then (this is the crucial and often forgotten step!) you will need to take your diary and **set aside some chunks of time** over the next few weeks to work through your chosen sections step by step at a pace that suits you and your lifestyle. Hopefully, the task of building emotional confidence will then seem much more manageable, and instead of feeling daunted or anxious you will have fuelled yourself with an inspiring emotion – excitement!

Enjoy the journey, and be generous with the breaks and treats!

Why We Need Emotional Confidence

For many of you reading this book, taking on the challenge of giving yourself emotional confidence may be the hardest kind of personal development work you ever do. By comparison, it is *relatively* easy to learn new skills (such as how to give professional presentations or dress in an eye-catching manner) and *relatively* easy to learn how to change specific aspects of your behaviour (for example, giving and taking criticism in a constructive and effective way). But to reach the point where you *feel* confident that you will always have enough emotional control to be able to *use* this learning whenever you choose can be a much harder (and a more lengthy) process.

I first became aware of this fact when I started teaching assertiveness training. I was thrilled to find this new technique of helping people. Its strategies were quick to learn, great fun to teach and, as I knew from my own personal life, undoubtedly effective. People would leave my courses on a great 'high' because in eight short sessions they had acquired the social tools which everyone else around them seemed to have and which they had longed for all their life. They now had a bag of tried-and-tested 'tricks' to ensure that they could make their voice heard, and stop others in their tracks when they put them down or didn't respect their privacy or rights. But after a while I began to notice that many people couldn't use these amazing new tools simply because their emotions stopped them from doing so. They would tell me that, although they knew their assertive strategies would work, they often felt too frightened, too guilty, too angry, too ashamed or even too choked up with love and compassion to use them. Later I found that exactly the same blocks would get in the way of people using many other personal and social skills which they fully accepted could transform their ability, for example, to be a better parent, more efficient at their work or closer to their partner.

Unfortunately, for many of the people I have worked with I have found that it can take much longer than eight short sessions to build the kind of emotional confidence they need to 'underpin' all their other personal development work. For someone whose problems are rooted in painful childhood hurts or persistent faulty mental programming, it can take two or more years to notice a substantial improvement. Compared with the length of time it may have taken for their problems to develop and their expected lifespan, you could easily argue that this recovery period is not in reality very long. But I certainly know that it often *feels* too long to the person struggling in the heat of their own emotional battlefield.

I've written this following list to remind you of all the rewards which emotional confidence can bring. Read it now to give your motivation an immediate boost, and then at any time when 'the going gets tough' and you may be tempted to give up on the challenge you have set yourself.

25 Compelling Reasons for Building and Maintaining Emotional Confidence

You can expect the following benefits from having sound emotional confidence:

1. Increased *self-respect*
   because your feelings are not 'making' you act in ways which are against your values
2. Firmer sense of *personal identity*
   because you can be more consistent in the way you react and behave

3. An ability to *use your brain more efficiently*
   because you will have better concentration, a more efficient memory and be able to switch more easily between your left, logical brain and your right, intuitive and emotional brain

4. Sustain your *motivation*
   because you can readily kindle positive feelings to keep you excited about your goals, and control negative feelings from intruding on your progress when you meet setbacks

5. *Save time*
   because you can make quicker decisions and get into action more rapidly by curtailing unnecessary worry and panic

6. Make *better decisions*
   because you will be aware of the influence of your feelings on your reasoning powers

7. Become a *better team-player*
   because you will be able to communicate more effectively and maintain your 'working' relationships in better order, containing any feelings (such as envy) when necessary

8. Be more able to *work on your own successfully*
   because you will not fear loneliness and will know how to keep yourself charged with positive emotion

9. *Thrive on change*
   because you can control the inevitable emotions that accompany you through both welcome and unwelcome transitions

10. *Take more risks*
    because you know you can think through consequences without being hampered by your emotional reasoning, and can be confident that you can repair your own hurt and disappointment if you should make a mistake

11. Be *more persuasive* in asking for what you want
    because you summon up just the right degree of appropriate emotion to give extra power to your message and 'hook' your audience

12. *Save money*
    because you do not *need* to become dependent on expensive stress-relievers such as alcohol, nicotine or 'crash-out holidays' to revitalize or repair your shattered nerves, and can work more effectively

13. Have the *friendships you* want and need
    because you can manage the fear that often accompanies making the first approach, or the guilt that is often triggered when you finish a relationship if it's no longer meeting your needs

14. *Love* and *care* more freely
    because you can trust that your heart will not override your rational mind, are able to heal yourself should you be hurt by the relationship, and are immune to emotional blackmail

15. Have a more *rewarding sexual life*
    because you can 'let go' knowing that you can control your passion when you want to, and are not too frightened to ask for what you want!

16. Be a *better parent*
    because you can be more consistent and stable in the way you give love, and more in control of your negative emotions so that they are less likely to hurt your children when they cannot defend themselves. Also you will be better able to help them develop emotional confidence through your role-model and informed guidance

17. Have *better physical health*
    because your nervous and immune systems are linked, and pent-up tension from mismanaged emotions puts a strain on your muscles, heart and most other organs

18. Have more *control* over your *eating habits*
    because eating disorders (eating too much or too little) are largely caused by feelings which are out of control

19. *Drive more safely*
    because you can keep calm under pressure and control your frustration and your responses to other people's 'road rage'

20. Increase your chances of *winning arguments and resolving conflict*
     because you have a better chance of being heard when you can put your case across with 'passion' while still maintaining control and the ability to think in a rational manner
21. Take more enjoyment from your own and others' *creativity*
     because you have freer access to the creative powers and sensitivity of your right brain. You can also allow yourself to get 'carried away' by art and music in the full knowledge that you can regain control and rational thought when you choose to do so
22. *Have more fun*
     because you can be spontaneous and give free rein to your excitement and humour, knowing that you can harness it again when you need to 'settle down'
23. Be treated with *more respect*
     because you don't make a fool of yourself or lose your dignity by allowing your heart to rule your head
24. Be offered *more support* from others
     because you won't burden them with 'overwhelming' emotional needs
25. Have more chances for *long-lasting success and happiness*
     because you can stimulate positive feeling which enable you to see the opportunities rather than the problems that fate puts before you. You can also make fuller use of your intelligence and skills, and increase the odds of your chances of *enjoying* a longer life.

I hope you are now well and truly convinced and longing to get down to the WORK!

Three Keys to Building Emotional Confidence

Key 1

Tame Your Temperament

– with Emotional Understanding and Skill

Understanding How Feelings Work

I hate driving. It's not so much the stress that upsets me as the boredom and, more importantly, my lack of confidence when I am behind the wheel. The main reasons behind these uncomfortable feelings are that a) I know virtually nothing about the workings of the machines I drive and b) I am completely dependent on others to help me out should anything go wrong.

Because I am aware of these limitations, I rarely take the driving seat. When I do, I always restrict myself to routes where I know I can readily get help, and I proceed at a very cautious safe pace.

I bet some of you have started thinking 'No wonder she gets bored and no wonder she's such an unconfident driver!' But I would argue that my car is by no means essential to my health, welfare or happiness, so I am quite content to maintain this level of driving confidence and to remain dependent on the knowledge and skill of others to transport me from A to B.

In contrast, I would *never* again accept being equally ignorant about the emotional machine within me. I am glad that I have now acquired sufficient knowledge about its inner workings to feel free to drive it wherever and whenever I want. I enjoy being able to 'rev' its engine up and down to my heart's content and still feel competent and in control even when I am driving my feelings at full throttle. Should this particular 'engine' break down or show any signs of wear and tear, I know how to repair it myself, quickly and efficiently. Although in a major crisis I might one day be happy to turn to professionals for some extra wisdom and support, I'm certainly glad I no longer have to run to them for every minor emotional wobble.

I am not suggesting that everyone needs my level of emotional knowledge to be able to run their own feelings with confidence. But I do know from my work in the self-help field what a tremendous support it can be to have, at the very least, a DIY level of emotional understanding. I have therefore written this section to give you a basic summary of the knowledge on the workings of our emotions. In order to help you assimilate the facts I suggest that you do the Instant Exercises as you read through the pages that follow. By personalizing the information and rekindling some of your own emotional experiences you will substantially increase your chances of remembering it.

If you'd like to extend your study even further into this fascinating area I have listed a number of excellent books in the Further Reading and Resources chapter (beginning on page 200) – which could keep you busy for the next year or two!

What *Is* an Emotion?

Having unsuccessfully scoured the dictionaries and psychological literature for a simple, concise definition, I've taken up the challenge to write my own. That's how I've come to understand why it was so difficult to find one!

Emotion is not easy to define or describe because it is a description of a series of complex, inter-connected 'happenings' in a number of different locations in the body and mind. The task becomes even more awesome when you realize that emotion can be described as either a *personal internal experience* or as a series of *scientifically observable facts*.

My final attempt at a definition is perhaps still a little too wordy for my own liking, but the examples and details given below should help to bring it to life:

An emotion is a **set sequence of responses** automatically triggered by the brain in order to prepare the body and mind for **appropriate action** when our senses perceive that something **relevant to our well-being** is occurring.

Why Do We Have Emotions?

The reason which evolutionists have given for the origin of emotion is that, as animals grew in sophistication, their young needed a longer period of parenting to safeguard their survival. The emotional bond between mother and child ensures that both *act* in ways that will mean that the young are less likely to be abandoned until they are fully capable of surviving by themselves. Interestingly, scientists have found that the brains of the very earliest of animals, the reptiles, are totally devoid of emotional neurons. On birth, baby lizards, I am told, instinctively stay motionless to avoid being instantly eaten by Mum. In contrast, today's young humans, with their sophisticated emotional brains, seem to know instinctively how to take actions which tug on Mum's guilt strings to keep her hovering around for a lifetime!

But of course, emotions can do more for us than ensure we get protective bonding with a parent. They also *help us to make decisions and act in ways which will sustain other key relationships*. As life on earth has progressed, we humans have become faced with more and more choices concerning our means of survival. Emotions may have been designed in part to stop us becoming paralysed by an otherwise overwhelming array of options. For example, it is thought that love and jealousy are the ways nature devised to help us select and stay in a long-term, stable relationships to rear our young when social and geographical mobility greatly extended our choice of mates. Similarly, shame and guilt may have evolved to keep us tied to specific sets of people. Being bound by a shared 'restrictive' value system means that we are more likely to stay working co-operatively while we are completing the kind of complex tasks which modern civilization requires and which cannot be undertaken by lone individuals.

So, in short, the reason we have emotions is to *motivate us to take actions which will be beneficial to the maintenance of our well-being and the survival of the human race.*

What Is Happening in Our Bodies When We Feel an Emotion?

Our emotional responses start their lives as soon as one or more of our senses detects that **something is happening (either internally or externally) which could have some bearing on our well-being**. This 'perception' by one or more of our senses sets off a kind of trigger switch in our brain, which then sets in motion a complex chain of physiological changes designed to make us react and act appropriately. For example:
– my *eyes* see a juicy ripe orange → the weather's very hot and I'm 'dying of thirst', so I feel *excited* → my mouth waters → my hand *moves speedily* to grab the orange before anyone else in the crowded room can get to it

Jessica's drawing opposite illustrates the route this feeling response travels as it passes through the different centres in our emotional brain.

Instant Exercise
Think of an emotional response you have had in the last couple of days and imagine its journey from its trigger through to its action.

Now let's take a more detailed look at information on the two parts of our emotional brain which have most relevance for our emotional confidence – the neocortex and the amygdala.

What Is the *Neocortex* and What Exactly Does it Do?

This is our **sophisticated comprehension centre** situated in the limbic system surrounding the stem of the brain. It is made up of a complex set of layers of neural circuitry, similar to the inner

workings of a sophisticated computer. It evolved originally from our ancestors' primitive 'nose brains', when smell was the only tool they needed to help them distinguish between what was good and what was bad for them. As humans developed they began to need a more refined sensor, so ever-inventive Mother Nature duly produced the neocortex.

This amazing piece of grey jelly-like substance has now evolved to such a degree that it provides us with a high-speed analytical decision-making and opinion-forming service. Its intricate web of nerves enables us to feel feelings about an event plus think through ideas about the kind of action we could take in response.

The neocortex also controls our emotional signal system, which enables us to 'hook' the emotions of others so they are more likely to give us what we need. For example, on our demand our neocortex will produce an appealing smile in order to seduce the passions of a fanciable mate, or an angry scowl in order to generate fear in an unwelcome trespasser.

Instant Exercise
Think of an emotional signal you have asked 'asked' your neo-cortex to produce in the last day or so in order to get something you need or want from another person.

What Is the Amygdala and What Is its Function?

The amygdala is another important centre in our emotional brain architecture. It is situated in the pre-frontal lobes, just above the brainstem at the base of the limbic ring – the central terrain of our emotional lives. Like the neocortex it is also a web of nerves, but it has a much simpler structure. It is, in fact, our original primitive emotional brain. It evolved as a mecha-nism for getting early humans speedily into fight-or-flight action when danger was sensed. Nowadays it is linked to the neocortex which, *most of the time*, acts as its command centre.

Once a significant event is sensed, the neocortex analyses its emotional meaning, decides which response is most apt and then sends instructions to the amygdala to generate appropriate action in our hormonal and muscular departments.

A) our eyes and ears sense a man running towards us who then trips on a banana skin and falls flat on his face

→ our neocortex thinks through the event and decides pleasure is the appropriate emotional response

→ it sends a message to the amygdala to activate the production of some *endorphins* (popularly known as our 'happy hormones') which then fuels our muscular system into action to produce a *smile*, and/or our throat to produce a *laugh*

B) our eyes and ears sense a man running towards us who is waving his hands to attract our attention

→ our neocortex thinks through the scene and decides that this man could be a nuisance to us and that *anxiety* is the best response

→it sends a message to our amygdala, which then activates the *pituitary gland* to produce a little *adrenalin* to *divert blood* from our skin in order to *feed our heart* and make it pump harder so our *muscles have extra energy*; we can speed up our pace and cross the road while at the same time screwing our *facial muscles* into a mildly 'scary' scowl

Why Do We Still Sometimes Respond Primitively?

Recent research into the workings of the amygdala has been very revealing. It is now known that if one of our senses 'thinks' that it has spotted a serious threat to our survival, our neocortex is bypassed and an emotional signal for action is sent directly to the amygdala. To fulfil this particular emergency service the amygdala keeps its own store of the following information:

i) past memories of emotional experiences
ii) pre-programmed blueprints of emotional responses which have previously been used with some success

Once an 'emotional emergency' signal has been received, the amygdala immediately scans its archives to match the key elements of this new experience with ones that have occurred in the past. Once it has found a 'good-enough' match it sets off the pattern of action responses.

It is particularly relevant for our purposes of building emotional confidence to realize that our amygdala's 'archives' include:

- a wide range of very primitive ancient memories and responses which have been imprinted on our genes over many centuries
  - we may have our cavemen forebears' favourite flight response for approaching spiders stored alongside our Victorian grandparents' choice freeze response for sexual innuendo!
- memories of our own most powerful and most frequently repeated past emotional experiences, plus the pattern of action which we previously used to respond to these
  - if we had repeated unhappy experiences as a result of change in our childhood we may have a blueprint of a 'childish' fear response to any new experience programmed into our amygdala

Instant Exercise
Think of a an emotional experience in your own childhood that still influences the way you sometimes react today, especially perhaps when you are under stress.

What Bearing Can the Amygdala's Emergency Function Have on Our Emotional Confidence?

There already seem to be many significant findings in this area of brain research, which is still in its infancy. Below I have listed the ones which seem to have the most relevance for our purposes. After briefly summarizing each, I have added a note on how this knowledge can be applied to some everyday emotional situations.

Instant Exercise
As you are reading each of the following sections, try to add an example from your own experience.

● The most dominant emotional memories are the ones which aroused the most feeling at the time when they were recorded in the amygdala.

■ This means that events which in the past have given us (or our ancestors!) the biggest scare or biggest thrill are highlighted in our emotional brain. They will be the first memories to be spotted during the amygdala's emergency scanning process – even though they may have no direct relevance for the current situation.

▲ The fast approach of a large crowd of people into a hall or lift or onto a station platform may reactivate emotional associations with being lost in a busy supermarket as a young child – or with the stampede of an army that threatened one of our ancestors!

● The earlier in life that memories are imprinted, the more likely they are to become permanent rapid-action blueprints which the amygdala will choose to apply in stressful situations throughout our lives. The very latest methods of photographing the brain have apparently revealed that highly emotionally-charged experiences (such as child abuse) actually make a physical impact on the architecture of the neural structure.

■ This means that under stress we are more likely to respond automatically with behaviour learned in childhood when we experienced similar emotions.

▲ A normally assertive parent may find him- or herself inappropriately obsequious and passive in the face of a child's critical teacher.

● Trauma in adulthood can also imprint emergency responses into the amygdala. This has now been given the label 'post-traumatic stress disorder' (PTSD). Research has confirmed that when a major trauma is experienced, new neural emergency circuits are sometimes set up.

■ This means that the pituitary glands of people suffering from PTSD are constantly over-worked and that it is much more difficult for them to reach a state of relaxation.

▲ Survivors of major disasters will often find themselves responding to minor emotional problems many years after the event as though these were major emergencies, and will find it very difficult to control their anxiety responses. This behaviour often makes it difficult for them to hold down a job or maintain relationships.

● When feelings are running deep, the amygdala automatically takes over. As it only has a limited choice of primitive, blunt fight-or-flight responses, the action it will initiate is bound to be either aggressive or passive.

  ■ This means that it is extremely difficult to be assertive or maintain a win/win approach when our emotions are highly aroused.

  ▲ A normally shrewd manager could become unwisely impatient if his or her anger is aroused during a negotiation process.

● The amygdala is incapable (unlike the neocortex) of coming up with new ideas or adapting to new applications and new situations. It therefore often provides out-of-date and inappropriate responses.

  ■ This means that even the most confident, capable and creative adults often respond predictably when they perceive themselves to be threatened.

  ▲ A medium-sized parent may impose unenforceable restrictions on a rebellious large-sized teenager as though their relationship had backtracked 10 years.

● The amygdala can initiate action much more quickly than the neocortex. Its instructions to the other parts of the brain to produce the necessary chemical formulae and set in action appropriate motor responses are sent in a matter of milliseconds.

  ■ This means that, although evolution has provided the neocortex with a 'damper switch' to curtail inappropriate activity in the amygdala, in an emotional emergency it has no time to use it because the amygdala is faster off the mark.

  ▲ At the sound of a sudden loud crash we can find ourselves shouting (maybe just like our parents or teachers) at an innocent child who tripped and accidentally pulled the table-cloth when we would have preferred to respond in a more nurturing fashion.

● After a 'silly', inappropriate amygdala response the neocortex goes into action to make sense of the response.

  ■ This means that we automatically start to rationalize our behaviour as soon as we are aware that we have made an emotional mistake.

  ▲ Attributing the blame for our own embarrassing and regrettable outburst to someone else's 'impossible personality' or the 'state of the kitchen'.

An Embarrassing Tale of My Amygdala Beating My Neocortex to the Finish!

This true story is a good illustration of my own amygdala leaping into action without consulting my higher brain.

One weekend I was walking with my husband in the depths of a large deserted forest at dusk when we heard a noise which sounded similar to a loud growl. Here's my understanding of what must have happened internally – all within a split second of time and all without my conscious consent!

My amygdala picks up an auditory signal (*'Howl'*):
→ senses its relevance to my well-being (*'Start emotional response'*)
→ scans its emotional memory-bank and finds a pre-historic memory (*'Prowling wild animal!'*)
→ scans for blueprints and finds one (*'Wild bears in deserted forest approaching unarmed fragile creatures!'*)
→ reads instructions (*'Stay still, stay quiet and make hasty retreat!'*)
→ declares emergency and sends message to direct limbic system (*'Crisis! Flight response required urgently'*)
→ message to motor response department (*'Freeze limbs for .25 seconds please!'*)
→ message to eyes (*'Open wide and scan field for best route out'*)
→ message to the pituitary glands to secrete increase of adrenalin (*'Give extra strength to heart, lungs and legs as soon as eyes find route'*)
→ message to sweat glands (*'Open up – let perspiration out – skin needs cooling'*)
→ message to heart (*'Beat faster and divert blood supply to legs'*)
→ message to respiratory department (*'Expand lungs and inhale deep breaths of oxygen'*)
→ message to legs (*'Set in motion and head speedily back to civilization!'*)
Two minutes later, when traffic from nearby road is heard:
→ message to all emergency centres (*'Crisis over, fragile creatures now in sight of safety zone – relax and resume normal functioning'*)

→ neocortex takes over the action (*'Try and make sense of that!'*)

→ major analysis of emotional concoction (*relief* – at not going to be eaten by wild animal; *embarrassment* – it was a forest in Hampshire – not a jungle!; *disappointment* – at being deprived of peaceful walk; *anger* – at self for reacting in such a ridiculously primitive manner; and *guilt* – due to jibes at husband for not being more reassuring)

→ sends an action message to my speech centre (*'Talk about the experience to husband, as he did an instant about turn too.'*)

→ incident concludes with neat rationalization (*'It wasn't that silly a reaction – after all there is a zoo nearby – it could have been an escaped animal: remember the story in last month's paper!'*)

A couple of weeks later when I was dipping into my literature on emotions to prepare for writing this chapter I was reminded that my primitive response has a long and noble history. It has saved the lives of countless generations of my protomammalian ancestors, so perhaps I should start being proud of it and more understanding when it makes the odd mistake!

Instant Exercise
Think of a similar embarrassing tale of your own (you don't need to publish yours!).

How Long Does an Emotion Last?

Psychologists say that the life of an emotion is very short – usually only a few brief seconds, and at most several minutes. They believe that emotions which last longer than a few minutes are in reality a number of different individual sets of recurring responses.

What Is a Mood?

A mood is a long-lasting emotional state which can be identified by specific patterns of biochemical and hormonal change.

It is experienced as a much less intense sensation and sometimes we may not even be aware of what is going on. A mood can last for hours or it can stretch over a period of days. An emotional state which persists for longer than a few weeks is called an *affective disorder*. This is a general term which you might hear used in connection with a sad or black mood which has developed over time into a depressive illness.

One of the differences between a mood and an emotion is that, when we are in a mood, our feelings and biochemistry do not necessarily correspond with any easily identifiable trigger. This is why we sometimes think that moods arise from 'out of the blue'. In fact they have always been induced by one or more of the following factors:

1. very deep emotional experiences which have not been expressed (e.g. through 'soldiering on' as though nothing has happened after a big disappointment and then finding ourselves in an 'unexplainably' snappy mood)
2. a number of quickly repeated emotional experiences (e.g. a series of frustratingly ineffective phone-calls leading to a despairing mood; meeting a succession of inspiring people at a conference or party leading to a motivated mood)
3. changes in internal chemistry due to, for example, lack of sleep, menstruation, food deprivation, weather conditions, etc.

One of the dangers about moods is that they can change the way we start viewing the world in general without our even realizing it. We start unconsciously selecting opportunities and people that fit in with our mood. So if we are job-hunting in a foul mood we tend to see only the jobs we are not likely to get, and to seek advice or consolation from cynics. The consequence being that our life can drift into becoming as genuinely 'foul' as our mood.

Instant Exercise
Recall a mood you have been in during the past week, and think about the exact factors that may have caused it. Note the

quality of the thoughts which you had while you were in that mood and whether they affected any decisions you made during that time.

What Is Temperament?

This is the term used to describe a particular person's predisposition to certain emotions or moods. Our temperament also affects the way we learn to express our feelings, so it can have great bearing on the development of our personality.

We experience and observe temperament as our habitual 'life-long' feelings which seem to be integral to our identity. We often talk about them guiding our behaviour and our attitudes. For example:

I'm a worrier → you won't see me smiling when there are too many changes around

I've got a bit of temper → I usually stay quiet if I see trouble brewing

I'm extrovert like my Mum and her Mum → we're always the noisy ones at a party!

READY-MIXED
☀
TEMPERAMENT
(LONG-LASTING)

CONTENTS:
GENETIC INHERITANCE,
PHYSICAL BRAIN STRUCTURES
LIFE EXPERIENCES

subject to environmental
conditions

Our temperamental patterns are set by a mixture of the following factors:

> – our genetic inheritance (e.g. a family can have a history of men who suffer from depression, or of women who are emotionally 'explosive')
> – the physical structure of our brains (e.g. someone who has been born with emotional damage to their brain in a specific area may be described as 'being quick-tempered' because that section of their nervous system cannot control their feeling responses very efficiently)
> – our life experiences (e.g. a person whose childhood was peppered with disappointments often develops a pessimistic temperament)

Instant Exercise
Write down three adjectives which are often used to describe your temperament; think if any of these might have been affected by any of the above factors. What kind of moods do each of these temperamental factors tend to encourage?

How Do Emotion, Mood and Temperament Relate to Each Other?

Emotion, mood and temperament are closely interrelated. I have listed some facts about their interdependence below. To bring this theory to life I have followed each with a positive example of its potential impact on someone chasing a life-dream.

Our imaginary dream-seeker is called Sophie. You'll notice that she is brimming with an enviable amount of emotional confidence.

Tame Your Temperament

Our temperament influences our goals

Sophie is an optimist by nature so she sets herself a challenging New Year goal – to find the love of her life!

Our goals affect our well-being; our temperament affects the actions we take to achieve these goals

She sets about energetically achieving her goal because she believes she will succeed and is confident that she can handle any disappointments she may meet en route

Our emotions are triggered by events which affect our well-being

Sophie feels happy when she meets someone who invites her to a party where she might achieve her goal

A series of the same emotions affects our moods

She is in a good mood because many good things have happened (over the course of the day) which have helped her to feel continuously happy (she achieved her target at work; the sun shone; she had a wonderfully tasty lunch and she heard the news that 105 bachelors had been invited to the party!)

Our mood influences the way we notice events which affect our well-being
Our biochemistry makes us susceptible to emotions which relate to our current mood

Because she is in a good mood, Sophie doesn't notice the rain and howling wind on the way to the party
She is in an exceptionally good mood because she believes that she stands a fair chance of imminently achieving her goal; so instead of getting depressed about all the gorgeous competition around her, she feels calm and confident – when a stunning guy beams at her from across the crowded room

We are more likely to sustain an emotional response when we are in a mood which is in harmony with the emotion we are feeling

Sophie now feels a trickle of energizing excitement infiltrating her happy, calm mood. As an optimist who thrives on challenging goals, and totally confident that she can manage any amount of passion, she begins to … … … …!

Instant Exercise
Note down a goal which you have achieved or would like to achieve. Think of the role your own temperament and moods have had, or could have, on the realization of that goal.

Does Each Emotion Have Its Own Neurological Response?

The short answer appears to be that we don't know. The only significant information I have gleaned from the research done so far seems to me to be glaringly obvious:

– negative emotions (such as anger and fear) arouse automatic nervous responses by pumping extra adrenalin into our system
– positive emotions (such as happiness and contentment) seem to do the opposite

The latter can 'undo' the physiological changes produced by the former, and bring the body back to a position of stable homoeostasis[1]

What Role Does 'Nurture' Play in Shaping Our Emotional Responses?

Once again we are in a difficult area if we are searching for proven facts and scientific laws. There is still much disagreement, between both psychologists themselves and between psychologists and other experts in this field. From my own practical involvement I am firmly convinced that the impact of our life experiences (i.e. 'nurture') does have a very great bearing on our emotional selves.

There are four main areas where nurture seems to play a significant part in shaping our emotional experiences:

1. *Helping Set the Threshold Point at Which Emotions Are Habitually Aroused*

For example:

> – how many times you need to be let down before you will tend to feel despair
> – how loud someone has to shout to make you feel frightened
> – how little needs to be happening before you will usually begin to feel bored.

As noted already, our individual threshold points will in part be fixed by our biological and genetic make-up but, as we know already, our emotional responses are also heavily influenced by the personal meaning we give to the triggers which send the signals to our brain.

So although some of our judgements concerning what is good or bad for our well-being are instinctively made (most animals will immediately feel fear when they are physically attacked), the vast majority have been formed by our life experiences.

To illustrate this factor let's look at the reactions of two people from different countries to a rainy day. As an English person I might not even notice the weather until the afternoon; then I might shrug my shoulders and feel mildly disappointed. On the other hand, one of my friends from the parched land of southern Spain might instantly become excited and feel constant pleasure throughout the day as his ears pick up the sound of raindrops.

The point at which emotion is triggered in each of us by the rain would be determined partly by our cultural temperaments but partly by the significance we have learned from our experience of life to attribute to rainy days according to their potential impact on our well-being.

There is yet another factor which can have a bearing on our emotional threshold: the sense of personal power we have regarding the rainy day. Let's imagine the rain was preventing us both from doing something special which we had planned for the day. I might feel instantly frustrated by my powerlessness against the elements. My friend's response might be to stay calm and pray for sunshine. Because he has been taught to believe that he can do something about changing the weather, his threshold for emotional arousal on this occasion would be much lower than mine.

Instant Exercise
Think of another example. Recall (or imagine) a time when you have been working with a friend or colleague from a different cultural background and your progress towards a certain goal has been blocked. Note the different points at which your feelings were aroused.

2. Defining What We Expect from Emotions

Our expectations about what emotions can or cannot do must primarily be learned by our experience of life. For example:

– someone whose mother cried freely and always recovered well from loss is less likely to feel frightened when hit by grief than someone whose mother locked in her feelings and, as a result, remained bitter and lonely all her life
– someone who attended a school where the head teacher used excitement about future career options to induce motivation will have a positive view of its power; another may view it much more sceptically because, throughout her life, she has been continually let down by experiences which initially seemed exciting.

Instant Exercise
Choose two contrasting emotions and think whether your life experience has left you with any positive or negative expectations about each.

3. Helping Shape the Style We Use to Express Emotion

Nowadays it is fairly generally accepted that our parents have a major impact on the development of our personality. Our emotional style is also significantly influenced by many other factors in our formative years. For example, the cultural habits of the country in which we live or the religion which we practise will play their part in influencing the manner in which we express our feelings. Most countries and religions develop rituals, customs and ceremonies which they use for expressing emotion. Some stereotypical examples:

- the Irish will express some of their grief through singing and dancing at 'wakes' for the dead
- the people of Saudi Arabia express their collective disgust for serious crimes of theft by watching the offender's limb being amputated in public
- in Italy one way mothers have historically learned to express their love for their families is through providing them with sumptuous, extended meals
- in Britain traditionally fathers often express their love to their sons by taking them to football matches.

So children learn to pick up a style of expressing emotion by watching the habits of the majority of people around them as well as through the role-models of important parent-figures. Even more importantly, they reinforce that learning by copying this behaviour and trying it out for themselves.

Of course, even with the same national culture each individual can have differing opportunities to practise their emotional skills, and this will also affect their style. For example:

- in many countries girls do not get as much encouragement to demonstrate anger or even to take part in situations (e.g. fighting, the stock exchange) where you would normally find triggers to this emotion. So, even if it is normal in their country to shout and bellow out frustration, women will be much less likely to do so than men

– although pride might be nationally regarded with disdain, in some families it will be considered more of a 'sin' than in others. The children of these families will be even less likely to share their pride in their successes

– in some school gangs where showing fear meets with disapproval, its members may not be as open as other children in expressing their anxieties about exams or punishments

– in some professions drinking alcohol is the normal way to deal with frustration, so its members are less likely to develop the skill of expressing anger openly but safely.

Instant Exercise
Think of two emotions and then consider how the style in which you express each has been affected by your opportunity to practise doing so.

4. Influencing the Way We Make Use of Emotion

I said earlier that one of the advantages of having a more refined neocortex is that we can use emotions as tools to help us survive and thrive. For example:

– if our mother tended to use 'emotional blackmail' to get us to do things we didn't want to do, we are more likely to use indirect ways of 'hooking' other people's compassion to get our needs met

– if we saw our uncle bullying his staff in his everyday business dealings with them, we are more likely to be tempted to use fear to motivate others

– if we have suffered a series of setbacks in the past we may have learned how to channel disappointment into new, positive activities and make it eventually work to our advantage

– if we have read a good deal of romantic poetry we may have become very skilled at how to pull heart strings through the careful use of language.

Instant Exercise

Name two emotions which you use successfully to help you get what you want in your everyday work. Think about how you have learned to make good use of these particular feelings.

Can We Have an Emotion without Realizing We Are Experiencing it?

Yes, there is now good evidence to suggest that Freud was right to confront us with the emotional life of our unconscious selves. The physiological stirrings of an emotion usually take place before our neocortex registers it, and it can simmer around below our threshold of consciousness as a hidden mood from hours to years.

Even if we are not aware of it happening to ourselves, the amateur psychologist in most of us will often recognize it in others. I am sure you must have been witness to one of the following examples either in your real life or through a film or book:

– the mother who for years has put her family's needs before her own, being unaware of her building resentment until she meets the sympathetic ear of a waiter on holiday!
– the young man who didn't realize he was falling in love with a colleague until his best friend started dating her
– the girl who doesn't realize she is embarrassed by a compliment until her boss asks her why she is blushing
– the man who is unaware of his fear of heights until the moment he is about to do a Bunjie jump for charity
– the woman with a history of sexual abuse who is totally unconscious of her deep feelings of shame until a therapist points to her bulimia as possible evidence of self-disgust.

Interestingly, I have just read in today's newspaper a very apt quote on this subject from a famous footballer. Having started counselling sessions, he talks about how he has now become aware of 'the rage inside me which had been building up for years'. There will be hundreds of sceptics smiling cynically at this 'confession', but equally there will be many millions who'll find his explanation highly plausible. The acid test is, of course: now that he has the emotion in the care of his conscious mind, will he take responsibility for it and learn how to express it safely?

Instant Exercise
Think of an example of when you were suddenly made aware of an emotion you didn't realize you had. If you cannot think of one for yourself, think of an example for one of your friends or colleagues.

What Happens If We Do Not Physically Release an Emotion?

Emotions are designed mainly to help our bodies prepare for appropriate short-term action. If that action (i.e. the expression of the feeling) is suppressed, the brain will tend to go on producing the hormones which generate the action appropriate to that particular feeling. The result is that the body may be kept in a physiologically aroused state for too long a time. For example, if we don't let go of our feelings of fear after a fright, our heart will continue its fast beating, our facial muscles will remain in a screwed up position, our shoulders will stay arched and our spine remain tightened long after the trigger which produced our fright has disappeared. All this unnecessary activity causes a terrible strain on our physiological system. There is now a substantial body of research evidence which indicates that this 'stress' does untold damage (often irreversible) in the long term and that it also affects our immune system's ability to fight off viruses and other infections.

The good news is that we also now know that by altering the way we think about what is happening or has happened we can sometimes switch off the brain's emotional response. In my experience this only seems to work if we do it in the early stages of an emotional response. Once a response has become 'set-in' for a long period the brain does seem to require some appropriate physical expression of the feeling before it stops its activity. We will be looking at this in more detail later on, and I will be giving you some tips on how you can both alter your thinking and give safe physical expression to your feelings.

Are Emotions Contagious?

Yes, they often appear to be unless people make a conscious effort to prevent themselves being 'infected'. I am sure you too have experienced one or more of the following:

> – finding your mood change from depressed to happy after spending time with a person who has just had some good luck or good news and is feeling very positive
> – watching a placid, fearful child become excited at a party full of extrovert, lively friends
> – being affected by the feeling which most other people are expressing in an underground, train carriage or lift when there is a breakdown.

People who have been held hostage for long periods of time often talk about their struggle to stay positive in the face of other peoples' despair. Those who survive the experience well, such as John McCarthy, have usually made a conscious effort to take control of their feelings and re-direct their minds onto positive thoughts and memories.

Instant Exercise
Think of an occasion when you had your mood quite radically changed by being in the presence of people in a contrasting emotional state.

Do We All Have the Same Experience of a Particular Emotion?

'Definitely not' is the concise answer to this one. Although the difficulties which people encounter may be similar, the way they respond varies enormously. So every solution to personal problems has to be worked out individually. In a world where so many other things have become standardized and predictable, I find such a challenge inspiring. I hope you do as well, because in order to build your emotional confidence you will most certainly have to adapt all the advice and tips in the rest of this book to suit your own unique emotional experiences!

Skills for Taking Control

Now that you have a reasonable idea of the workings behind your emotional engine, it's time for a driving test!

We cannot begin to develop emotional confidence unless we know that we have, at the very least, the minimum level of skills to ensure that we can stay in control of our feelings in action. If you are keen to drive in the emotional fast lane of life and open up your throttle to deep passion and thrilling excitement, you'd be well advised to aim for advanced standards. But for the moment, why not see if you are fit enough to cruise competently with more everyday feelings?

I have prepared the following checklists so that you can review your competence in the three areas where you need to have good control: your body, mind, and behaviour. Have a notebook and pen handy – I suggest you pause between doing each checklist (and perhaps reward yourself!).

Checklist 1: How Good Is Your Control Over Your Physical Responses?

Breathing

On feeling fear, anger or excitement, should you find yourself beginning to hyperventilate (breathing shallowly and quickly from your upper chest), can you quickly return your breathing back to its normal pattern?

If not, it's time to practise some deep breathing exercises. These can be learned from most stress-management books and courses, any Yoga practitioner or a physiotherapist.

Muscle Tension

Do you have a technique (other than taking a painkiller) which you use on a regular basis to release built-up tension (e.g. headache or backache) which has been caused by having to hold in feelings?

If not, learn one quickly and practise it daily. Simple techniques such as tensing and relaxing each muscle individually can be learned from cassettes. If they fail, you could try consulting a specialist such as an Autogenic Relaxation trainer. Here's one of my favourite Quick Relaxers.

Instant Relaxation

Close your eyes. Uncross any crossed limbs and check that your body feels firmly supported. As you breathe in deeply, imagine that through every pore of your body you are taking in relaxing energy in the form of white light; pause for a brief moment, and then, as you breathe out, imagine that you are releasing a warm orange glow through every pore. Do this several times until you feel your limbs are free of tension, and then allow your imagination to take you to one of your favourite relaxing places. Absorb the scene for a moment, and then focus your mind's eye on one specific object while breathing naturally and easily for about five minutes, letting your body feel lighter and lighter. I always focus on the fountain in our garden in Spain, but you could equally well use the face of someone you love, a treasured object or a favourite flower. If you do this relaxation technique regularly over a period of time, you will eventually find that you can get an instant sense of peace just by closing your eyes and bringing your object into your mind, because your brain has formed a neural connection between this image in your memory and its relaxation response.

Can you name one aromatherapy oil which is known to induce physical calm, and one which has the opposite effect?

If not, take yourself to the aromatherapy stall in your chemist, or sign up for an evening class and treat yourself to a burner or some appropriately scented candles.

Do you do some physical exercise at least three times a week which gives you an opportunity to discharge pent-up energy and tension?

If not, make a date with your sports centre, buy an exercise video, borrow a dog to walk or (if you're like our family and you need a push) get yourself a personal trainer!

Diet

Can you name six kinds of foods and three drinks which create unrest in the body and heightened activity in the mind?

Can you name 10 foods and three drinks which you always include in your diet when you know you are likely to become emotionally fraught?

If not, consult a dietitian, read a book on the subject or visit your local health food shop.

Catharsis

Can you name three ways which you regularly use to give expression to your positive feelings?

If not, book a seat for a comedy show once a month; take a trip to the Fun Fair; take dancing lessons and get yourself a hug!

Can you name your favourite safe (and socially acceptable) way of giving physical release to the following feelings: fear/mild frustration/anger/disappointment/sadness?

If not, buy a squeezy stress ball; find a cushion which can stand a thump; get some voice training; buy a CD of 'weepy' music (I have one of weepy extracts from the classics) and stock up on tissues.

Professional Help

Can you name three kinds of professional helpers you could turn to should you need an extra dose of stress-relieving therapy?

If not, consult a directory of complementary medicine practitioners or the appropriate listing in your Yellow Pages.

Checklist 2: How Good Is Your Control Over Your Mind's Responses?

Can you name three common irrational thinking habits which people tend to use when they feel depressed or under stress?

If not, learn my GEE Strategy immediately! (Photocopy page 39 and pin it up in a prominent place.)

The GEE Strategy

GEE is a reminder word, made up of the first letter of the key word in each of the following questions. If you hear yourself thinking or talking negatively, ask yourself these three questions. You may find that you are feeding your mind unnecessarily with anxiety. You can also use it to challenge (mentally or verbally) other people's negative talk when it is disturbing your peace of mind.

a) Am I *Generalizing* from one or a small number of incidents? – for example, am I saying that 'Public transport in this country is dreadful. You can never rely on it' in response to one bus being late, while the reality is that only three out of the 50 buses I have been on this month have been late?

b) Am I *Exaggerating*? – for example, when I say 'I've been asking you all evening. No one ever listens to me. I might as well talk to a brick wall' am I saying the whole family or the whole office never listens to me, when in fact most people here do take me very seriously and most of the time they do respect my requests?

c) Am I *Excluding* positive aspects or possibilities? – for example, on hearing that there is going to be a re-organization of my department at work, is my response 'That must mean my job will go' or 'That'll mean more work in half the time.' Challenge a blinkered negative outlook by focusing on the possibility that this news could mean more efficient working and less stress for everyone.

Can you name two other positive thinking strategies which you use whenever you need to curb a negative feeling?

If not, read a book on positive thinking (there are some examples in the Further Reading chapter), or talk to people who are positive thinkers and ask them for their tips. Devise some relevant Affirmations for yourself immediately and promise to use them for the next month.

Affirmation Technique

Affirmations are positive self-talk statements which we say to ourselves on a regular basis to counter repeated negative thoughts and feeling. Although it seems a very simplistic technique, it has proved to be highly effective in countering negative childhood programming patterns. If you say them regularly they will begin to pop automatically into your mind during an emotional emergency and can have a very calming effect.

During a particularly tough emotional time you can write a few affirmations on cards to keep by your bedside and read just before you go to sleep or as you wake in the morning (times when your subconscious is more accessible). Alternatively you can record them onto a tape and play them as you are travelling to work or as part of your normal morning routine.

Affirmations are most effective if you use the first person and the present tense and stay within the realms of possibility!

Examples:
I am calm and in control
I am a calm person
I am in charge of my fear
I enjoy my anger and I use it safely and constructively
I have control over my excitement
I am loving
I am a highly compassionate person

Note: You will find more examples in the BALM exercises for each emotion in 'Harness Your Habits' (beginning on page 99).

Can you recall two dreams which highlighted an emotional problem you had, or which helped you to become more aware of a feeling in your subconscious that needed your attention?
If not, start jotting down your dreams as soon as you wake up, and see if you can spot the feeling behind the images. Share your dreams with people whom you know and trust. You don't have to accept their interpretations, but just talking often does help us achieve insight. If this fails, buy a book or see a counsellor who specializes in dream work.

Can you name three objects or pictures which are symbolic of negative feelings for you, and three which stimulate positive feelings in you?
If not, take a walk around your house and find some. Treat yourself to a small new object which will have positive significance for you and which you can carry around with you when you need it. (Pavarotti has a simple white handkerchief to help him feel good and calm his nerves when he's doing a major performance, so you don't need to spend a fortune!)

Do you have a favourite quotation or saying which you use to motivate yourself with positive feeling whenever you feel sluggish?
If not, treat yourself to one of the encouraging quotation books listed in the Further Reading chapter (*page 200*), or take a look at some of the quotes in the BALM exercises in the chapter entitled 'Harness Your Habits'.

Can you name one way in which the technique of Creative Visualization could be used to help build or boost your emotional confidence? If not, it is highly likely that you don't know what I am talking about! This technique is one of the most useful ways I know to prepare yourself emotionally for a situation which demands that you keep your feelings under good control. My self-help version is below. I have named it 'The Prophetic Pacifier' because if you do it well, what you imagine *does* come true!

If you find it impossible to do this on your own, seek help from a counsellor or self-help group which uses similar techniques. Alternatively, there is a book by Ronald Shone listed in the Further Reading chapter which offers a useful introduction to the technique.

The Prophetic Pacifier

This technique uses Creative Visualization to help you prepare yourself emotionally for a difficult event. It involves feeding your subconscious mind an image of you doing whatever you want to do in the calm, confident manner you would like. Because your brain cannot distinguish between a real event and an imagined one, it registers the experience in its memory-bank under the file: 'Been here before – no problem/Emergency emotional system not required.'

You can use it the night before your event or just before it – or both, for a double dose!

What you will need:

- peace and quiet – if you can't get it easily, try ear plugs and an eye mask
- soothing background music
- a supportive chair, a comfortable (but not too soft) bed or a warm bubble bath
- aromatherapy oils to burn or put in your bath (not essential, but a helpful extra).

Lie, or sit, in a well-supported position. Close your eyes, take three deep slow breaths and spend five minutes or more getting yourself into a deeply relaxed state. When you have reached the 'floating' stage and your body feels light, use your imagination to visualize yourself stage by stage, calmly preparing for your event.

Then, as though you were watching a film, in your mind's eye see yourself going to your event in a relaxed manner, and then handling it in the most confident, calm way you can imagine. Make your image even more vivid by focusing on the details of what you are wearing, your exact facial expression, and the rest of your body language. Listen with your mind's ear to your strong, controlled voice, using exactly the language you would like to use.

Watch the reaction of the other people in the room to your confident and calm performance.

FEEL and savour the feelings you have as you watch yourself acting with superb emotional confidence.

Gently return yourself to reality and open your eyes.

(Depending on which kind of music you choose – uplifting, inspirational, etc., you can adapt this visualization to different situations, for example to induce a state of controlled enthusiasm or excitement.)

Do you have a technique to help you when you are getting anxious (and possibly distraught) because your mind is going around in circles and you cannot think straight?
If not, learn some helpful creative thinking techniques (described in my book *The Positive Woman*, and in Tony Buzan's book *Use Your Head*) when you are in this emotional state, such as Brainstorming and Mind Mapping. Alternatively, do some 'arty' doodling, a meditation to stimulate your creativity, or revive your thinking powers by doing some quick 'Brain Gym' exercises designed to stimulate cross-lateral thinking (i.e. thinking with both sides of our brain, the analytical left side and the creative and emotional right side).

Brain Gym

Lazy Eights
Draw the figure eight horizontally in the air or on paper with each hand eight times, and then with both hands together three times.

Cross Crawl
March slowly for five minutes touching the knee of each leg in turn as you raise it with the elbow of your opposite arm. (It has been found that this exercise, if done regularly, helps to establish new pathways between the two hemispheres of the brain.)

Checklist 3: How Good Is Your Control Over Your Behavioural Responses?

Can you name three things that you must do before giving a presentation or a talk to ensure that your voice doesn't let you down through anxiety or excitement?
If you cannot, read a book on presentation skills or enrol on a course which will give you some practice.

Do you blush when someone pays you a compliment?
If so, then you need some extra practice in learning to respond with a simple 'Thank you'. The way to ensure that you receive more compliments is to start giving many more (but only genuine ones, of course). Ask a friend to help you using simple role-play, or use Creative Visualization to help you see yourself taking compliments calmly and confidently, without blushing.

Can you name three body language signals which are commonly used to express these emotions: Fear/Anger/Happiness/Frustration/Compassion/Contentment?
If not, start observing and asking around. Find yourself a good book on body language, or sign up for a Communication Skills course.

Can you name three variations in the ways body language is used to express the same emotion in different countries?
If not, read a good book on cross-cultural communication – or go and see your travel agent!

When you are particularly anxious about a meeting, are you always too late or much too early?
If you are either, get yourself a time-management diary and practise some relaxation techniques.

Do you find negative emotions arising purely from poor personal organization, such as an untidy office or an untidy home?
If so, get organized! Start every day with a 'To Do' list, and reward yourself each time you complete it. (Make sure it is always an achievable list, because the rewards will motivate you!)

Do you get flustered and stay quiet or get annoyed and snap back if someone criticizes you?
If so, learn to do some role-play exercises in giving and taking criticism, or do the self-help exercises in my book *Super Confidence*.

Do you clam up or behave 'wimpishly' when you need to make a complaint? Do you feel anxious about making a complaint?
If so, learn some assertiveness skills. There are many books on the subject (*see the Further Reading chapter*). As a taster, read the following exercise on one of the most useful self-protective techniques, and remember there are many more where this one came from!

Broken Record
A self-protective assertiveness technique

Aim of Technique:
- to aid persistence in making a justified request or complaint and retain emotional control

When to Use:
- in situations where yours or others' rights are not being respected
- when you need a quick response, and do not want (at this moment or ever) a lengthy discussion or argument
- when the other person is getting over-emotional
- to bring a meeting back to order, or to the agreed agenda
- when you want to move the other person towards accepting a compromise or negotiated settlement

When Not to Use:
- to resolve complex interpersonal problems
- when you are unsure of your rights
- when it would be unsafe for you to annoy the other person

Method:
- Choose one or two short sentences to summarize the situation and what you want.
- Repeat one or both 'Broken Record' sentences over and over again.
- Use a relaxed body posture and a calm, firm tone of voice.
- Either ignore, or quickly acknowledge with an empathy statement, arguments, pleas, emotional blackmail, 'red herrings', protestations, distracting questions or asides, etc.

Example:
(Note: Jill's Broken Record is in *italics*, while her empathy statement is in **bold**.)

Jill: The deadline for submission is August 30th – *I must have the figures by Friday.*

Barry: That's impossible. I'm up to my eyes in work this week.

Jill: **I appreciate that it is difficult for you**, but *I must have these figures by Friday.*

Barry: Can't you hang on until next Wednesday? I could look at them over the weekend.

Jill: No. *I must have these figures by Friday.*

Barry: Don't you think this job is difficult enough without being put under this kind of pressure.

Jill: **I know there are many difficulties with your job Barry, and I hope the pressure eases off soon**, but the fact remains that *I must have these figures by Friday*.

Barry: Oh, OK if you insist, but we're going talk over these ridiculous deadlines in the next project meeting.

Jill: Fine, that's a good idea – thanks a lot.

Do you start behaving in ways which you would prefer not to when you are angry or are faced with someone who is angry?

If so, you need some anger management skills. Find a course or read my book, *Managing Anger*. Here is my favourite quick-fix technique to tide you over in the meantime.

'Don't Get Too Boiling'
A quick-fix strategy to cool your anger

This strategy should be used as soon as you feel your anger beginning to take a physical hold (e.g. your pulse quickening, muscles tightening, head throbbing, etc.) Learn this mnemonic off by heart immediately!

Don't	Get	Too	Boiling
I	R	E	R
S	O	N	E
T	U	S	A
A	N	I	T
N	D	O	H
C		N	E
E			

Examples

The technique can be used in a wide variety of situations. How you apply it will depend on a variety of factors, such as the degree of anger you are feeling, where you are, and whether or not you are able physically to leave the situation which has triggered your angry response.

- Distance
  - – let go of any physical contact; take a step back; lean back in chair; leave the room.

- Ground
  - take hold of some firm inanimate object; bring yourself back 'down to earth' and into left-brain mode by some distracting observation such as counting all the blue objects in the room or the number of circles you can see; do a mundane chore; think of the shopping or the recipe for tonight's meal.
- Tension
  - clench and unclench fists; screw your face up and release slowly; curl and uncurl your toes; thump or kick a cushion; shake your wrists; scream.
- Breathe
  - use your favourite breathing exercise to calm your pulse; make sure that you continue to take deep, slow breaths for at least the next five minutes.

End of the driving test, you'll be pleased to know! How did you do?

If you found that your skills were inadequate or very rusty, make yourself an achievable action plan. List the skills you want to learn or upgrade in order of priority for you, and note down beside each what action you need to take plus the date when you will check that you have done the task you've set yourself. Don't be tempted to procrastinate with this important personal work – these skills are vital for your emotional confidence. Most are very easy and often fun to learn, but, just like any other skill, they require practice on your part to keep them in tiptop condition. A friend and colleague of mine who leads *Positive under Pressure™* courses with me sums it up well:

> *The process of developing skills to build up our emotional strength is just the same as we use to build physical strength. It usually involves doing exercises more often than we want, more regularly than we want and for longer than we think is necessary.*

DR MALCOLM J. VANDENBURG

So, while you are learning and practising these skills, don't forget to give yourself plenty of encouraging treats, rewards and support to boost your motivation!

[1] adapted from Levenson, in P. Ekman and R. J. Davidson, *The Nature of Emotion* (OUP, 1994)

Key 2

Soothe Your Sensitivity

– with Effective Emotional Healing

In this section I will be introducing a strategic approach to emotional healing which can help us to recover more thoroughly and more quickly from hurt, disappointment and loss. It is just as effective for old emotional wounds (from as far back as our childhood days) as for the knocks we may receive in our present-day lives. It can be used with minor hurts as well as major ones.

In Great Britain we have a grand old tradition of buttoning up emotional pain and psychologically soldiering on. This 'old guard' attitude to hurt has infiltrated the consciences of many individuals who, even when they are deeply wounded by emotional hurt, ask questions such as:

Aren't we all becoming too soft and soppy about emotional pain – surely fortitude and time are all I need?

Aren't most pleas of emotional distress just convenient excuses to evade responsibility?

Why should I heal? Wouldn't a life of flat, colourless and stagnant happiness be worse – I may be hurting internally, but at least with my pain I feel alive?

What right have I got to spend time, energy and money on giving myself therapy when there are so many millions of people still fighting for their right to subsistence and a tolerable degree of physical health? They have to put up with much worse, so why should I complain?

Hopefully you are already convinced, as indeed I am, that unhealed emotional wounds are as potentially dangerous to our health, welfare and happiness as their physical counterparts.

But just in case your conscience is prodding you about this, or you are still harbouring some doubt for any other reason, let's begin by looking at the damage some 'everyday' emotional wounds can do if they are ignored and allowed to fester.

You will note that some of the examples that follow are much more severe and destructive than others. They all have one thing in common, however: each caused an intolerable amount of unnecessary damage simply because it was allowed to fester in an unhealed state for too long.

As you read this section through, try to match each of my examples with at least one from your own experience.

Five Good Reasons for Healing Emotional Wounds Promptly and Efficiently

While we are in a state of emotional pain, whatever the cause and however old the hurt:

1. We Have Less Resistance to Other Hurts

Jill, a marketing consultant, is jilted by a lover. To preserve her 'pride' she has decided to ignore the hurt and bury herself in her work to distract herself from her inner pain. A week later she is giving a presentation to a customer which is strongly (but quite legitimately) challenged. Under normal circumstances this is a situation in which Jill is renowned to thrive. But today the criticism fails to trigger her usual assertive response – instead it adds a dose of salt to her wounded pride.

The order is lost and her confidence is doubly shattered by her deep sense of disappointment in her 'professional' self.

2. We Are Likely to Be More Fearful of Potentially Good Opportunities Which Could Be Emotionally Strengthening

Jim's mother left home when he was 10. He was the oldest of three children. In the practical chaos that ensued, and amid the demands of the highly distressed younger children, his own silent sadness was hardly noticed. By the time his distraught father found the energy and time to give him some attention, Jim had built an emotional wall around his heart. He denied feeling sad and abandoned, and 'bravely' resisted all further attempts by both his father (whom he adored) and sympathetic teachers to give him the comfort he so desperately needed.

By the time he was 36, Jim had a trail of over 200 shattered short romances behind him, and a Christmas-only relationship with his family. His confidence in his ability to manage an emotionally rewarding relationship was virtually extinct.

3. We Can Experience Emotional Confusion, Caused by Inappropriate Feelings Leaking into a Current Situation

Sarah is very excited about an interview for a senior position she has been wanting for several years. She has been specially recommended and called for interview by the boss. She is well prepared and reasonably confident in the knowledge that she has an excellent chance of being given the job. She performs well and is more than satisfied with the terms and conditions, so she is thrilled when, at the interview, she is offered the job.

But as she is leaving the room, she is aware of a sick feeling in her stomach. Her heart begins to palpitate and she feels shaky. Thoughts of self-doubt begin to flood into her mind. (*It's one thing being able to talk myself into the job, but how can I live up to their expectations?*) She's thrown into a state of emotional turmoil and her confidence in her ability to do the new job has plummeted.

This is a familiar emotional state for Sarah. She feels it every time she is on the brink of success and happiness. It first started when she unexpectedly failed an 'A' level and could not do the course of her dreams. No one else in the world knew how hard this failure had hit her. In fact, everyone was amazed at how lightly she appeared to take the setback and how quickly she settled down to her job as a clerical officer, even though it was the kind of work no one would have dreamed she was destined to do.

Even though Sarah knows the origin of her sabotaging feeling, she still cannot control it because her original hurt has not yet been healed.

4. We Are in Danger of Losing Control If a Feeling from an Unhealed Wound Is Echoed and Inappropriately Amplified

Brian has had a hard day at the warehouse. The roads have been in chaos all day and almost every delivery has been late. His boss has been in a foul mood and refuses to hear any explanations. Brian knows there was little point trying to defend himself. It just makes matters worse. He has learned to take the 'water off a duck's back' position.

His route home is equally frustrating – the traffic still chaotic. Just as it becomes clearer and Brian is at last able to put down his foot, a car cuts in front of him, catching his side mirror in the process. Brian immediately 'flips' into an out-of-control rage and sets off at breakneck speed to teach the other driver a lesson he'll never forget.

Ten minutes later John is flagged down by the police for speeding and reckless driving. His anger takes an abrupt turn inwards and he arrives home in a depressed, sullen state, denying that anything is the matter. A miserable evening is had by all.

5. We Endanger Our Ability to Feel and Express Positive Emotions Such as Joy, Excitement, Love and Compassion

Linda is thrilled to hear the news that her sister is getting married. She loves her deeply and knows she has found the perfect partner. But when she is told that they have chosen a low-key wedding with only one bridesmaid (her sister's best friend), she is deeply hurt. She is ashamed of her own reaction and shares it with no one. She feigns complete support and understanding for her sister's decision and emphatically denies any disappointment.

When two years later her sister rings to tell her she is pregnant, Linda finds she cannot take much pleasure in her sister's excitement. She reflects sadly on how they seem to have grown apart.

Can We Heal Every Emotional Wound?

Some emotional hurts cut so deep that, just like their physical counterparts, they are bound to leave long-term or even permanent scarring or weakness. Jim's desertion by his mother at an impressionable age is an example. Another one is my loss of my daughter Laura. This is a wound which I and my family know we will have with us for the rest our lives. My emotional healing 'goal' in relation to this devastating loss is not complete recovery. I would not expect to (or even want to) be able to reach a stage when I no longer feel any pain. So I have to choose a goal, which I consider to be realistic, that is to heal well enough to be able do what I want to do with the rest of my own life. I know that I want to reach a stage when I can be in sufficient control of my underlying grief that it does not undermine my confidence in my ability to support my other daughter and my husband, to use my skills as a writer and therapist and to lead the work of Laura's Foundation.

Why Are Some People More Adept at Emotional Healing than Others?

In my twenties I used to look with envy and wonder at those people who seem to bounce back more easily than others from emotional knocks. Each one I received battered and bruised me more deeply, until eventually I was too psychologically weak to take any more and I had the inevitable 'nervous breakdown'.

Now *I* am one of those people others envy. I do not attribute this turnaround to a quirk of nature. (To my knowledge, I've received no injection of magic psychologically-strengthening genes!) I know it has happened because I have now *learned* how to heal myself from emotional hurt, and have made a *habit* of putting this learning into practice in my everyday life.

Inspired by my own personal experience as well as my success in my work with others who have been similarly hurt, I began to take a special interest in finding out exactly what was involved in the healing 'process'. What I began to notice was that, although the causes of our hurts were wide-ranging (e.g. childhood abuse, school bullying, failed exams, redundancy, marriage break-ups, put-downs from colleagues and friends) our blocks to healing and the 'treatment' we needed to overcome these were very similar.

Naturally, I also researched widely on the subject as well, and listened to many other therapists' experiences and observations. I then noted and compared the very specific actions which we had taken on a wide range of recovery journeys. I listed which of these had helped and which had hindered. And, just as my colleagues specializing in grief counselling had identified some clear stages in the 'healthy' recovery process after loss, I also found that a step-by-step pattern was emerging. From this I was then able to develop a self-help tool which I now call the *Emotional Healing Strategy*. It is a seven-step guide to the most helpful actions you can take to encourage and support the natural healing process at each of its different stages. As I said earlier, it can be used on everyday small hurts as well as the major ones. It can be used with very old emotional wounds even if the feeling appears to have died or has never yet been sensed.

How Can this Strategy Help Build Emotional Confidence?

Over the last eight years of using the strategy, I have found that it can strengthen emotional confidence in two main ways:

1. It is a handy *diagnostic tool*. It helps us to understand why our efforts to recover after a hurt are not being as successful as we would like them to be, and points up which *specific changes we may need to make in our behaviour and habits* to meet our emotional needs more effectively.
2. It is a reassuring *practical planning tool* which we know we can depend on. We can use it to *guide us rationally* along a sensible healing path in the aftermath of a hurt. It is in these stressful moments that our old, unhelpful habits are most likely to re-emerge.

During the last 18 months since Laura died, I have found the strategy has helped me many times to get 'back on track'. As I find myself beginning to slide back down into my black hole of hopelessness, I now hear a calm, pragmatic inner voice saying:

'Come on, now remember the strategy. Let's use it to see what's going on. Something's obviously wrong. You've got stuck again, that's all. Perhaps you're rushing yourself. You know this is a wound which will be re-opened again and again, so just be patient. So what if you have to go back a stage or two? You *know* that you'll naturally move on again when you're ready – you've done it many times and you'll do it again. You of all people know the consequences of not swallowing your own medicine!'

The Emotional Healing Strategy

I will soon be taking you step by step through an illustrated guide to the strategy, but first it would be helpful to have a general overview.

As mentioned, there are a total of seven stages – but there is an important difference between the first five and the last two.

For any long-term effective emotional healing to take place, it is *essential* to work through the first five steps; being able to complete the last two is a *bonus*. In my experience, the last give us an extra boost of emotional strength and confidence while at the same time being very helpful to *other people* as well.

The Five Essential Steps:

1. Exploration – examining the exact nature of the hurt
2. Expression – releasing some of the feeling stimulated by the hurt
3. Comfort – taking support and encouragement from a source outside ourselves
4. Compensation – finding some way of being recompensed for the hurt
5. Perspective – examining the hurt in its wider context.

The Two Bonus Steps:

6. Channelling – using the experience of the hurt in a constructive way to help ourselves, others or the world in general
7. Forgiveness – absolving who, or what, was responsible for the hurt and putting it firmly behind you.

The order in which I have listed these is significant – it appears (from my own experience and through my work with others) to be the ideal sequence. Often the steps do overlap, as when we are near to completing one we often find ourselves quite naturally moving on to the next. But a golden rule would appear to be that *skipping steps very often leads to inefficient, 'phony' healing* (i.e. the kind that appears to work for a while, but often lets you down badly if you should meet a similar kind of hurt in the future).

I have devised a mnemonic to help you remember the first letter of each step in its correct order:

Every Emotional Cut Can Produce Creative Fruit

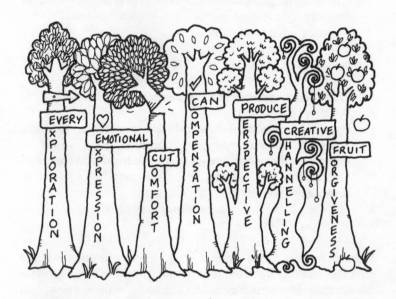

You may want to photocopy the drawing illustrating this and put it in a prominent place so that all the elements of the strategy become firmly fixed in your mind.

We will now consider each step in turn, with examples of positive action that could be taken for a wide variety of hurts.

Step One – Exploration

Our aim: *to acknowledge fully the hurt and use our conscious mind to examine our perception of what happened.*

In this first step it is very important right at the outset to remember that our focus must stay on our *personal experience*. For the purposes of this stage in the emotional healing process we are *not* interested in:

- the 'real' truth or proof
- anyone else's perception of what happened
- why it happened
- making judgements on the seriousness or otherwise of the hurt
- who or what is to blame.

The *key questions* we want to be able to answer are:

- What do I remember of what happened?
- What did I feel then?
- How did I experience these feelings? (e.g. knotted stomach, going red, shaking, crying, foot-stamping, going numb)
- How did other people react to my feelings? (Do I remember them protecting me, or acknowledging my hurt or helping me recover from it?)
- After the hurt, with what feelings was I left?
- What do I feel now?

Most of these questions might be quite easy to answer if the hurt has taken place relatively recently and has not been that devastating. But sometimes, and for some people, answering them can prove to be exceedingly difficult.

At some stage in our evolution, human beings developed a *psychological defence system against emotional pain*. This allows us to push memories which trigger difficult feelings from the fore-front of our conscious mind into the recesses of our subconscious. It is often an essential short-term survival mechanism. It enables us to *postpone the healing of our hurt* so that we can get on with coping with the practical consequences of the hurt, or just carry on surviving in spite of it. For example:

- being able to get on with funeral arrangements after a death
- looking after children if a partner has deserted
- marshalling resources for counter-attack, or protection, in the face of violation
- re-securing our property after a burglary

– continuing to earn a living after a setback or disappointment

– carrying on with a presentation after some unfair heckling or criticism.

Repression (its technical term!) is a brilliant emotional management tool, as long as the hurt is given healing attention in the not-too-distant future. The problem arises when it is used as an alternative to healing – of course, even more problems arise when it becomes a *habitual* way of dealing with emotional hurt.

So, as we begin our exploration it is important to remember that *the longer our feelings have been repressed, the more difficulty we are likely to have with this stage in the healing process.* This is especially true if our hurt has been very severe because, generally, *the more serious the trauma was, the harder it can be to recall the repressed memories.* This is why early childhood abuse and memories of horrific traumas such as the Holocaust can be notoriously hard to recall when they have been locked away in the backs of the victims' minds for decades.

Exploration in Action

There are very many ways of helping yourself work through this stage. Some of these can be done very quickly, while others may take weeks or even months to be effective if the emotional wound is deeply buried. Many of my suggestions you will be able to do very easily on your own, but a few may need the help and support of a friend or a counsellor.

The specific kind of action you may need, or want, to take will depend on both the nature of your hurt, the kind of person you are and the resources you may have available. Remember there are very few hard-and-fast rules. *The same hurtful event experienced by one hundred different people is likely to be experienced emotionally in a hundred different ways – and it could take a hundred different types of action to explore the impact of that same event!*

But here are some suggestions for action which I and others have found helpful. If they do not seem appropriate for *you*, perhaps reading through them will help you to think of something else you could do.

◊ Talk to a friend (but a patient, non-judgmental listener rather than an advice-giving talker!).

◊ Talk to yourself (!) – use the questions on page 58 as a prompt. It sometimes helps to speak out loud to an imaginary you seated on an empty chair. (But do choose to do this in the privacy of your own home or you run the risk of getting hurt yet again!)

◊ Consult a counsellor or therapist (but only one who agrees to work through your hurt in this way).

If you have a problem remembering:

◊ Use photos or any other significant objects (e.g. old toys, books) as a trigger for your memory.

◊ Talk to others who were around at the time (but only as a trigger for your memory – their views or feelings are not important at this stage).

◊ Play music from that era – put it on as background music – and let your subconscious make the connection (if you try too hard it won't work).

◊ Making sure that you are in a relaxed state first, use your imagination to play a scene in your mind of how you think it might have been. This sometimes helps the real events suddenly to 'click into place'.

◊ Revisit the scene of the hurt.

◊ Read a book or see a film or look at paintings on the same theme as your hurt.

◊ Talk to others who have had similar experiences (but remember at this stage that your goal is to explore *your* experience, not theirs). Also, don't be tempted to talk too generally or get into any intellectual analysis. There will be plenty of time to help others and make sense of the experience during the later stages of your healing.

◊ Paint, draw or sculpt an impression of what happened and what you felt.

◇ Join a drama group which does improvisation sessions. This will help free up your spontaneity and exercise your emotional (right-hemisphere) brain. Memories often suddenly emerge if this side of our brain is 'warmed up'; we then encounter or feel an emotion which is evocative of the hurt. A dramatherapy group would be ideal for this purpose, if there is one running locally to you.

Step Two – Expression

Our aim: *to experience, to at least some small degree, the bodily sensations of the feelings involved, and allow them some 'natural' and safe physical expression.*

Recently some psychologists and therapists (particularly from the cognitive schools) have been questioning the need for the release of feelings as part of the healing process. They claim that research has indicated that not only is it not necessary, but it can also be counter-productive because it can inflame feelings and make them harder to keep under control.

I have some understanding of this view because I have myself been witness to the harmful effects of undisciplined cathartic styles of therapy. When I first started to train and work in this area, these methods were so popular that it often seemed to me that the quality of the therapy was judged not so much by the long-term results, but by the number of decibels in the screams and tissues in the waste-bin. Being an introvert by nature and 'tongue-biter' by nurture, I found this therapeutic world very intimidating and was very anxious that I would never make the grade as a 'proper' therapist. But interestingly, I remained in awe of this way of working for many years in spite of seeing vast numbers of people opt out of therapy because 'they couldn't take it,' and many supportive relationships blown to smithereens because one party could scream and the other couldn't.

But I couldn't dismiss this kind of work either, because it was obvious that there was more than a grain of 'truth' in the cathartic approach. There were undoubtedly magic 'breakthrough' moments of healing for some people, which other methods of therapy had failed to make happen after years of effort.

Eventually after many years of experimenting with a whole variety of techniques, I found a style of working with Expression which felt comfortable to me and my particular clients, and was more suited to self-help therapy. Although I remain firmly convinced of the healing potential of being able to feel and release feelings, I believe that this should (ideally) take place only as part of a gently evolving step-by-step process which also includes many other therapeutic aspects (i.e. this Emotional Healing Strategy!).

Before reaching the stage where you can feel your feelings, many of you may have to 'go to battle' with your mental programming. Unfortunately, many modern societies have encouraged the suppression of difficult hurt feelings. Choking back tears and looking cool in spite of our anger or fear is often judged as courageous, and a symbol of strength and 'good breeding'. These cultural attitudes were in my case reinforced

by experiences in early childhood which 'taught' me that sup-
pressing my hurt feelings was sensible. At an early age I
learned that by expressing them I was putting myself in danger
of being shouted at, laughed at, hit or rejected, and I was likely
to hurt other people, emotionally or physically, whom I needed or loved. I also saw (and indeed felt) plenty of evidence that
when other people expressed their hurt, the results could often
be painful and dangerous.

So, like many, many other people I have now met through
my work, I reached adulthood thinking that even the safest and
most natural forms of Expression such as crying, trembling or
foot-stamping are:

- bad-mannered
- uncivilized
- childish
- unmanly
- unfeminine
- unprofessional
- hurtful
- dangerous
- sinful.

If my experience has started ringing bells, you too will have to
reprogramme your mind to think positively about this step. It
is likely that you too have not had enough *practice* in discharg-
ing hurt feelings. Like any poorly practised behaviour Expression may therefore at first seem unnatural as well as being
anxiety provoking, because it will feel 'awkward' as well as
'wrong'. Furthermore (as if you didn't have enough problems!), when you do first start to work on this step, you may
find that surges of repressed feelings leak out at inopportune
moments.

But do stay with it! I promise you the rewards will far out-
weigh any initial difficulties. Be reassured that, for this strategy
to be effective:

a) it is not necessary to experience a full-blown histrionic release of feeling, even if the hurt is worthy of such passion. *It is only necessary to make a small (easily manageable) degree of physical contact with the feeling.* So a trickle of tears, a pang of jealousy or a deep growl in the throat might be quite sufficient.

b) after working through this book and putting it into practice, *you will eventually be much more able to control the expression of your emotion*, even if more emotion than you thought was there did emerge.

When you first take a look at the following list of suggestions for action, you may find yourself feeling uncomfortable. At first it will almost undoubtedly seem very odd to be 'coolly' preparing a time to express your feelings. You'll probably start to mentally counter my advice. Unfortunately I won't be there in person to argue with you, which is very frustrating for me because you may skip on to the next chapter or close the book. So, in an effort to keep you reading, I am going to write a short account of how I imagine a discussion with the sceptical or embarrassed part of you might proceed!

You   *This is all beginning to feel weird and unnatural – you should-n't and you can't force feelings to come out like this.*

Me   *There's no force involved – we are just removing some of the familiar barriers (e.g. pressure of time/other people's opinions and feelings/distractions). Forcing feelings out leads to 'phony' feelings and that can make matters worse, not better. What we are doing is gently coaxing in a conducive, safe atmosphere. In these conditions, if emotion needs to be dis-charged it can, and will be – quite naturally. That's why old, unexpressed, difficult feelings have a nasty habit of coming up just as we begin to relax into a holiday and want to forget them, or just when we are cozily wrapped up in bed and want to get a good night's sleep.*

You   *But what if I go to all this trouble and then nothing happens?*

Me   *For a start, don't think there is anything wrong with you. Just trust that if you need to express the feelings, they will emerge.*

Maybe you'll learn that the feelings you think you ought to have aren't there. Around the time of my divorce, I made a special effort to arrange a safe time and place (a therapy session) to let go of the anger and sadness I thought I must be feeling underneath my calm exterior. I was surprised to find that no such feelings emerged. But my time, effort and money was not wasted because by giving myself this opportunity I did learn that relief and hope, not anger and sadness, were my dominant feelings. This insight (gained in the presence of people who knew me and my self-conning tricks well!) gave me a much needed boost of emotional confidence. As a result I became much more trusting of my ability to tackle the many inevitable problems that accompanied my new single parent status.

On the other hand, maybe you are just not ready to handle these feelings and it may take a little longer. For deeply buried, severe wounds it can sometimes takes years.

You   *But what if I get too deep into my feelings and I can't switch off?*

Me   *By the time you have read the following suggestions and worked through the rest of this book, you will have many more ideas to help you regain control. In 'Harness Your Habits' you will find lots of ideas on how to manage eight of the most difficult emotions, and in the Further Reading chapter I have suggested many other books which will also be helpful. Finally, remember Expression is only one step of the healing strategy. The release of feelings in the safe, gentle way I am suggesting, followed by the next three steps, does in my experience give us very much more, not less, emotional control. It is the feelings which are strangled inside of us until they reach bursting point that are very difficult to switch off.*

But I doubt whether I could ever convince you with 'talk', you'll have to test the theory for yourself. So why not give Expression in Action a try!

Expression in Action

You can work on Expression on your own, with a friend or in a small group. A group larger than eight should, in my opinion, be led by one particular person who is emotionally sensitive but very capable of managing his or her own feelings.

◊   Set aside some specific 'wallowing time' when you can feel free to express your emotion in whatever way you wish. Your time schedule should include an appropriate recovery period as well. If you are working on your own I would advise allowing at least one hour. If you are working with others, I have found that two hours is about the right length for such a session. A shorter time-span doesn't give you time to build up an atmosphere of trust and safety. A longer one can be very exhausting and it is much more difficult to control feelings when we are tired.

◊   Set aside a specific evening, weekend or week. The amount of time you will need will depend on the nature of the hurt and the degree of feeling you think you might want to express. Knowing this space has been set aside for your feelings to emerge will help you to contain them until that time and will stop you putting off 'doing it'. (This is easily done – who actually finds it easy to put 'feeling sad/angry/disappointed/angry' at the top of their priority list?)

◊   Give these 'sessions' a name. One person I know set aside one day a week for a couple of months while she was working through a difficult childhood hurt, and called this 'My Heal and Feel Day'. I thought this was a wonderful title, but if it doesn't appeal to you make up your own. Giving self-help expression time its own title could help you to treat it with the seriousness it deserves, and protect its space in your diary.

◊   Choose a place that feels comfortable, safe and protected from unwanted intrusion.

◊   If you have an answer-phone, put it on. If not, unplug the phone.

◊ Make sure you have any 'props' you may need ready. (For example, a box of tissues/tapes or CDs/a cushion which can be thumped/paper which you don't mind tearing.)

◊ If you are 'working' on your own and are at all worried about getting into feelings which you might not be able to switch off, let a friend know and arrange for them to ring or call at a certain time after your session, or meet you for lunch the next day. Doing this will help you to stop worrying about it and make you feel freer.

◊ If you are working with anyone else, discuss what you would do if one of you became overly upset or angry, but remember that often it isn't the person who has been expressing the most feeling who may need the most support afterwards. (Usually the person who has been able to let go feels much stronger.)

◊ Use music to set a conducive mood for expressing the hurt feeling, but also have some other choices handy to help you recover your calm and poise, if you think you'll need them.

◊ Burn some appropriate aromatherapy oils.

◊ Have a snack before you start if you are hungry (we are all more vulnerable to lose control of our feelings if we are hungry).

◊ Start by getting yourself into a physically relaxed state (*see page 35 if you need help with this*). Begin to recall the memories, using the power of your imagination to replay the hurt. Evoking the details of the scene can help (the colours, smells, facial expressions). If you are working with other people, try talking about the hurt in the present tense. Sometimes it helps if someone is gently making physical but unobtrusive contact with you while you are doing this (such as touching your hand or shoulder rather than enveloping you in a cloying hug).

◊ Don't try to force the feelings out, and remember that you only need to make some kind of physiological connection with the emotion for this stage of your healing to be effective. Remember to stay with the kind of expression which feels comfortable for you – howling works for some of us, but others may only need to feel a tremble in their stomach. (There are absolutely no extra bonus points for the loudest scream or hardest thumped fist!)

◊ Use objects which have a special emotional significance for you, to focus your attention on (a present from a departed love, a photo of the person you have lost, a letter which has upset you, a brochure of the company that has let you down).

◊ Have a nurturing treat ready for yourself at the end of your 'session' (a delicacy in the fridge, a good video or some special bath potion – but go very easy on alcohol or caffeine – they may give you a temporary lift but the 'down' that they leave you with afterwards is not good when we are in an emotionally raw state).

Those who do not know how to weep with their whole heart don't know how to laugh either.

GOLDA MEIR

Step 3 – Comfort

Our aim: *to allow our hurt self to be soothed by the caring attention and/or actions of at least one other person, who can accept and respect our feeling and demonstrate genuine concern for our welfare.*

If your hurt has been very minor, you may be able to complete this step on your own. Receiving a treat from the nurturing part of yourself may prove to be sufficient comfort. So if you have ended the last step as I suggested, you may have already gently moved yourself across the bridge into this healing phase. All you may need to do is to extend your treat!

Unfortunately this is much more likely to be the exception rather than the rule. Usually in order to work through Comfort you will need the help of at least one other person. On hearing this news, you may immediately start to feel anxious and find that excuses like the following start crawling fast and furiously out of your inner woodwork!

No one knows about it.
I couldn't tell anyone else.
I don't know anybody like that.
No one else could understand – how could I expect them to?
I could never ask.
I'm the strong one – they depend on me – they'd be upset.
I haven't time.
They wouldn't have time.
They've got enough on their plate.
I'd feel silly – that's just not me.
I'm a very private person.
I've never cried in front of anyone since I was six years old.
If they knew how jealous I felt, what would they think of me?
If they knew I had that kind of anger, they'd be terrified.
I can't afford to expose the vulnerable side of me.
I've asked before and been let down. Not again, thanks.
I don't need it.

I admit that I have personal experience of using many of these 'crazy' excuses to deny myself Comfort. (And yes, they do deserve that adjective because taking comfort after a hurt is both a natural and rational thing to do.) Perhaps they were not always verbalized so explicitly, but nevertheless variations on their themes inhabited my head until I was well into my forties! What a relief it was to rid myself of them. I cannot imagine surviving the loss of my daughter without being able to indulge myself fully in this essential aspect of emotional healing.

So before we move on to how you can encourage comfort, I'll give you some tips on how you can rid yourself of these hindrances.

How to Beat the Excuses

Stage 1
Look for the root cause of your self-sabotage. (There always is one, although sometimes it is easier for someone else to see through your resistance.) Then, of course, take some positive action to counteract it.

Here are some common examples. The solutions are prefixed with the symbol →

Root Causes of Resistance to Accepting Comfort

not being given comfort routinely after a hurt as a child	→backtrack on the strategy and heal that hurt
having been let down by someone who was supposed to be your comforter (e.g. an inadequate or abusive parent; disloyal friend; poor counsellor; hypocritical priest)	→heal that hurt
low self-esteem	→rebuild your self-esteem (see Further Reading)

neglected friendships (not giving enough time to maintain closeness)	→re-charge friendships
misjudging friends	→ask them when you are not in crisis about whether they would be willing to give you support
the wrong kind of friends (ones who only want to see the strong or fun side of you or could not understand)	→make new friends immediately
Not having enough time, energy or freedom to find an appropriate friend	→find a counsellor (and no, they don't all cost a fortune and many offer comfort at the end of a tele-phone line)
lack of assertiveness	→do some assertiveness training – the ability to ask for help can easily be improved with practice and encouragement

Stage 2
Check that you are looking for the *right kind of comforter*.

Once you have done battle with your excuses, you can start looking for the person or persons who can help you complete this step.

If anyone else has been present with you during the last stage of Expression, it may be that you already have some offers. It is believed that the universal body language of people who are expressing hurt evolved as a survival mechanism as humans became more civilized and inter-dependent. So, for example, cry-ing is not just good for releasing our tension, it is also designed to trigger caring, protective responses in other people in our social group, so that they automatically feel the urge to comfort and look after us and are automatically rewarded with that pleasant physical 'glow' for their efforts. ('Emotional blackmailers' spe-cialize in manipulating these bits of our biochemistry!)

Furthermore, the whole experience of giving and receiving comfort welds people together. For example, a family who have supported each other through a tough bereavement, or members of a community who have helped each other through a natural disaster find their sense of loyalty and commitment to each other strengthened. So, if and when an outside threat should come, the group is more likely to rally protectively as a closely united force.

Unfortunately, in the hectic, pressurized world that most of us inhabit, nature's built-in comfort response is having a hard time. The sad reality is that even though we may have conquered the problems of Expression and are quite able to show and express the hurt we may be feeling, we may be living the kind of lifestyle where our *'Help, I'm hurting'* signals are simply not noticed or, if they are, potential comforters inhibit their natural response to console or support. Even though I am a professional in this area, I have to admit that there have been many times when I have not responded to the non-verbal signals of others' hurt simply because I was:

- 'speeding in the fast lane' of my own life
- overly preoccupied with my own pain
- overly absorbed in enjoying my own happiness and good fortune.

I am not proud of this behaviour and I accept total personal responsibility for it, but I know it is not unusual. This is an important fact of modern-day life which comfort-seekers need to accept. In order to draw attention to our need for comfort *we can no longer rely on mother nature's signals to be picked up; instead we must learn to make assertive verbal requests to selected people.*

Many people I meet have become disillusioned and cynical about the possibility of getting comfort from other people simply because they have *a habit of asking the wrong kind of people*. Frequently they even have a history of asking people who are more likely to hurt them again than hold out their arms in sympathy!

I have therefore drawn up a list of characteristics of the *ideal* person to turn to at this stage. Even the most sensitive, kind human beings (being human) may not *always* meet these criteria, but we should be aiming to get someone who is currently able to fit the following portrait fairly closely, and not someone who doesn't come anywhere near the ideal.

Portrait of the Ideal Comforter
A person who:

- genuinely cares about you and your welfare (i.e. feels sincerely concerned or upset that you have been emotionally hurt)
- is able to communicate this caring clearly through **either** words or deeds (you shouldn't have to rely on mind-reading when you are in this state)
- is able to get 'in tune' with how you are feeling. **Even** if your comforter may never have had exactly the same experience, or if they did, had reacted differently, they must have felt similar feelings to your own in the past (e.g. 'I know how it feels to be let down. Although nothing quite as bad has happened to me, I did feel a bit of what you must be feeling when ...')
- can accept your feelings for what they are and doesn't feel compelled to tell you what you *ought* to be feeling (e.g. 'You shouldn't be feeling sad – you should be glad to be rid of her' or 'I don't know why you are feeling angry, it isn't *your* problem')
- can be non-judgemental with you and hold on to any thoughts they might have about any mistake you may have made (e.g. 'You had it coming to you, didn't I warn you?' or 'If you had been more careful')
- is emotionally confident (or, at the very least, doesn't go into flat panic at the mere thought of a tear or a raised voice!)
- is a good listener and able to hold back their own 'stories', news and advice, while you are working through this stage

- respects the level of bodily comfort you want (e.g. doesn't insist on a hug because that's what they need to give you)
- is assertive enough for you to feel sure that they will say 'No' when they cannot or don't want to help for some reason
- is strong and capable enough to protect and look after you during this period
- would be willing to support you when you move on through the next steps of the emotional healing process
- is the kind of person whom you would be happy to give Comfort to should they ever need it
- would not expect their kindness to be considered as a debt that needs repaying at sometime in the future
- is able and willing to take full responsibility for the repercussions that helping you might make on their own life (e.g. 'Don't worry. I'll do extra work at the weekend to make up the time,' or 'Don't concern yourself with her – if she gets jealous, I'll handle it,' or 'I can always grab a nap in the afternoon if I have a disturbed night, so ring me anytime')
- has the time, emotional and physical energy to give you the kind of Comfort you need

and finally,

- if you have been unjustly hurt, can feel anger on your behalf and express the anger you feel but cannot access at present. And can (with your permission) take protective action if perhaps you are still too stunned, upset or powerless to be able to do so.

Don't forget that the above is a portrait of an ideal comforter for emotional healing, and not a profile of a good friend, perfect partner or parent. Sometimes our nearest and dearest can fulfil this very specific role, sometimes they cannot. If reading the list has pushed your own guilt buttons, remember that even the most perfect of people cannot be the ideal comforter to all people at all times!

Comfort in Action

- to strengthen your resolve to *ask* for the comfort you need, remind yourself of the positive benefits to others of giving comfort. Spend a few moments recalling a time when you yourself have helped someone in this way or when you have witnessed someone else being healed by a good comforter.
- read the section on the ideal comforter and then take a look at the people you know who might be able to 'fit the bill'. Remember they may not be people who:
  - love you the most
  - you love or like the most
  - have given you comfort in the past
  - are currently offering you help
- *Ask* your chosen Comforter for help using assertive, direct language. Specify clearly the *kind* of Comfort you want and *how long* you think you will need it for. Remember, in some instances you may not even want to talk about the problem. Just being in their company and soaking up their sympathy or empathy could be sufficient. It is often a good idea to indicate what you *don't* need as well and that *it is OK for them to say 'No'* because that reassures some people who may fear they cannot cope. Here are some examples which I hope will give you an idea of the language that is most likely to get you the response you need.

How to Make an Assertive Request for Comfort

Examples:

a) after a disappointment at work: *'John, I've just heard that I didn't get that order – you know the one I have been work-ing on for months. Do you fancy sharing a pint with me tonight – I'm OK now, after sounding off about it all to Julie. I'm not going to burst into tears or anything, but I could just do with bending your ear for an hour or so. But, please feel free to say if you're busy – it's not that urgent.'*

b) asking a friend, after looking back at a childhood hurt: *'Jo, you know that film on TV last Sunday about that family where the mother was dying of cancer? It was very spooky for me. It sparked me off thinking about my own childhood and I've been really upset all week, remembering the time when my Mum died. I know I don't know you very well, but I know you had the same sort of experience and I'd just like to spend a little time talking to you about it because I think you'd understand. I'm not in a major bad way or anything – just feeling a bit raw and fragile. I wondered if you could come round for lunch one day soon. But please say if you can't or if it would be upsetting for you, I'd understand perfectly and I am sure I'd find someone else to help.'*

c) Asking an aunt and uncle, after the break-up of a rela-tionship: *'I think you've probably heard that Mandy and I split up last month … Yes, it's been a really tough time, but I feel as though I am now getting through. What I now need is a break from all the high emotion. I wondered if I could come and spend a long weekend with you both … Thanks, that would be great. A bit of a rest, some walks with the kids and some of your cooking is just what I need.'*

d) Asking a friend for moral support after receiving a redundancy notice: *'Would you drop round for a coffee for an hour on your way home? I'd just like to sound off to you about what happened. Everyone here has been great, they've* helped me, but they feel sad and are trying to cheer me up. I just need to blow off a bit of steam and I think you'd understand. If not tonight, perhaps another night this week ... Well, if you could get up a petition on our behalf that would be brilliant, thanks. We'll talk about it later.'

Now all that is left to do is sit back and soak up the healing power of Comfort. Replace any niggling worries about 'getting stuck' or 'imposing' with positive affirmations, e.g. 'I trust that I will naturally move on when I am ready to do so. _____ (your Comforter) can take responsibility for their own welfare.'

If grief is to be mitigated, it must either wear itself out or be shared.

ANNE SWETCHINE

Step 4 – Compensation

Our aim: *to make appropriate amends to ourselves for the hurt.*

By now, you should be feeling much better and you may now be thinking it is time to forget the past and get on with the present and future. If you are like many people I know, you may even be feeling a little guilty for indulging yourself so much over the hurt, or you might have started to get anxious about the backlog of things you need to do. The whole world may now appear to be peopled with saints who are getting by in life in spite of much worse hurts than you have had to endure!

But I hope you will persevere through this understandable resistance, because although you could survive without this step and the next, you will only do so in an emotionally weakened state. You are still psychologically fragile and therefore more susceptible to being wounded by any other hurt which may come your way.

This step will reinforce the healing you have completed already and is a vital link in the whole process. But before we start, let's clarify more specifically the kind of amends we are seeking for good quality healing.

In seeking Compensation for ourselves, we are *not* looking for:

- *revenge.* The thirst for revenge is a highly understandable reaction to being hurt. It is a deeply embedded instinctive survival response. But like many other primitive responses we still possess, it is not necessarily the most sensible one for humans to use today. We need to remember that it pre-dates the development of our cognitive capabilities, which are normally of much more use to us in terms of our current 'survival' needs. For the purposes of emotional healing, it is rarely useful, never essential and sometimes downright counter-productive!

  So, however strong your urge for revenge may be, at least for the moment put it aside. Turn your focus away from the person or thing which hurt you, and back on to yourself and your own emotional health.

- *just punishment.* Even if this is well and truly deserved and advisable, you will be much better equipped to take appropriate action when you are recovered. In some circumstances the wheels of justice may not be able to wait for your healing (e.g. after being a victim of a robbery or crime of violence, it makes communal sense to ensure our attacker is quickly apprehended). In such circumstances we must, of course, co-operate in doing just this as soon as possible. But at the same time we must not forget our own emotional needs and fragility. This is the time to lean on friends or professionals who can and want to help us. Working on this step at least gives us something to do, while others, who are emotionally less bruised, take up our cause. It is also a good diversionary activity should our anger or frustration kid us into thinking that we need to take the 'law' (written or unwritten) into our own hands.

– instead, we *are* looking for:

- a way of *recompensing our degree of hurt, whatever kind of deed (big or small) caused it.* We know that we all have our own individual way of reacting to different losses, injustices and disappointments. For example, the sudden loss of a much loved animal might be more emotionally wounding to some people than the loss of a parent. So we have to ignore the 'face-value' which others might generally give to our hurt, and judge for ourselves what kind of Compensation *we* need.
- *good-enough amends* in relation to our emotional healing needs and not perfect 'tit-for-tat' recompense for the damage. For example, if your hurt has left you with a serious physical disability or the loss of a key person in your heart, you would be right to think that you may never be able to find a perfect way of making it up to yourself for such a major loss. But that stark awareness should not (as it has done with many people I have met) prevent you from spending time at this stage looking for at least some degree of healing recompense.

- *a style of making it up to ourselves which suits our unique personality* and our preferences, even when our way of working through this step may seem odd and inappropriate to the people around us ('I wouldn't do that – it's just a waste of time. What I'd do is …!')

Compensation in Action

Think about the kinds of 'deficit' in your personality, skills, material needs or life opportunities with which this hurt has left you. Use this checklist to help start you thinking. You may realize that you have more than one deficit and therefore you may have to arrange different kinds of compensation to suit each.

Deficit Checklist
As a result of your hurt, have you been left with insufficient:

> self-esteem
> self-confidence
> optimism
> physical energy
> trust in other people
> trust in a specific kind of relationship (e.g. marriage or boss/employee)
> social support
> financial security
> opportunity to use your personal strengths
> opportunity to use your skills
> opportunity to develop your academic potential
> opportunity for fun
> inclination to have fun
> lack of social skills (e.g. assertiveness)
> other: _____

If, after completing this checklist, you have begun thinking (like many people before you have done) 'What's the point? I can't undo what's been done,' use positive self-talk to focus your mind back on what you *can* do. ('I *can* change the impact the hurt is having on my life' and 'I *can* give myself some recompense for the damage that has been done already.')

Choose an appropriate means to give yourself some recompense for the hurt. Remember that very rarely are you looking for an instant pleasurable treat (although admittedly, with smaller hurts, this kind of Compensation may be perfectly apt). This step, especially in relation to healing childhood hurts, could entail some long-term planning and some persistent work. There follow some examples which should help you to start thinking along the right lines.

Examples of Appropriate Compensation

Hurt	Compensation	Example
being let-down on a date by a friend/not getting an expected order at work/harsh unjustified criticism from a boss	a self-nurturing treat	aromatherapy bath/a meal out with a friend/a lazy evening in listening to you favourite music/a weekend break
divorce/enforced move to new area/chronic shyness due to over-isolated life as child/death of close friend or partner	make new friends	join a social club/sports centre/singles holiday/dating agency
years of being bullied at school/authoritarian father/rejection by a series of girl or boy friends	a self-development course	confidence building; communication skills

81

under-achievement at school due to family difficulties or disability/failed unusually difficult exam	academic learning	adult education; more reading; encyclopaedia – CD ROM
ambitious or selfish parents who failed to notice and develop innate creativity/authoritarian teachers at a school who only valued academic learning	creativity development	join a drama or creative writing group; art or writing class; learn to play an instrument or sing

When one door of happiness closes, another opens; but often we look so long at the closed door that we do not see the one which has been opened for us.

HELEN KELLER

82

Step 5 – Perspective

Our aim: *to gain an understanding of why and how the hurt occurred, and salvage a positive aspect from the experience which we can take forward into the future with us.*

Now (and only now!) are you ready to do some serious *thinking* about your hurt. It is hardly likely that I will have to do a 'hard sell' on the virtues of this step. In fact you have probably been itching to reach it for a long time!

In our highly-intellectualized modern society, many people make the mistake of trying to jump to this stage before they have completed the first four steps of emotional healing. I am sure you must have heard people who are still reeling in pain and shock crying out: 'WHY did he do it?' 'HOW could I have let myself get into that situation?' 'WHAT was going on that made this happen?' Months or even years later these same people could well be knocking on my therapy door, still crippled with emotional pain and still torturing themselves with the same questions. It is usually hard to persuade them to let go and backtrack through the early healing stages. They are full of impatience to complete this step because, perhaps through previous personal experience, they have learned how crucial it is for moving forward.

This job is made even harder if we are surrounded by a culture which expects instant healing and encourages fast-forwarding through this stage. (*'We're a business, not a charity. We have every sympathy but the show must go on. Learn from the experience and then think positive, look forward; the past is the past.'*)

If you have successfully worked through the last four steps, you are now more than ready to don your analytical cap and learn from the experience. You should *instinctively* feel you *want* to do it, rather than thinking that you *ought* to do it. Your heart is now healed sufficiently for the cortex of the brain to carry out its analytical duties efficiently.

But of course, for some hurts this may be easier said than done. Some are very hard to comprehend, because the situation surrounding them may have been very complex. Others may never make sense because those responsible for the hurtful deed may have been acting quite irrationally. Nevertheless, it is still worth giving Perspective your 'best shot'. Having done this, you will certainly feel better and should be able to give up distressing and exhausting yourself with unanswerable 'Why' questions.

The Five Tasks of Perspective

I have identified five main areas for action for this step, and devised a mnemonic to help you remember each, and their order:

Cut People Reflect Sensibly to Learn

1. **C**ontext — we examine the events leading up to and surrounding the hurt.
2. **P**atterns — we look for any repeated sequences and habits.
3. **R**esponsibility — we decide who or what was to blame.
4. **S**ignificance — we decide how meaningful this hurt is in terms of the 'big picture': the situation, relationship or our life in general.
5. **L**earning — we clarify the wisdom we have acquired as a result of this hurt, and assess how this can be used to benefit us and/or others.

For a small, 'everyday' hurt, all five stages may be able to be completed on your own in a matter of minutes. An older or larger, more complex hurt, however, may need months of time and could require the help of others.

Perspective in Action

Ask yourself the following questions on the five tasks:

1. Context
   - what was happening externally and inside me prior to the hurt?
   - what was going on when it happened?
   - which people (if any) were involved?

2. Patterns
   - have I felt hurt in a similar way before?
   if so, how often?
   - have the preceding events been similar or different?
   - were the people alike in any way?
   - were their words, body language or behaviour similar to previous hurts?

3. Responsibility
   - did any aspect of my behaviour or personality have a bearing on what happened?
   - was anyone else partly or wholly responsible?
   - were any other factors partly to blame? (e.g. weather, economic strain, prejudice, ignorance, illness, hormones, generation gap, fate)
   - who or what has the major share of responsibility?

4. Significance
   - on a scale of 1 to 10, how serious an impact did this hurt have on me and my life?
   - does it have any importance in relation to anyone else?
   - does it have any significance in relation to an issue which is of concern to me? (e.g. social, political, moral)

5. Learning
   - have I learned anything about myself as a result of this hurt and its effects?
   - have I learned anything about anyone else?

– have I learned anything about life in general?
– is there anything I can do from now on to protect myself from re-experiencing such a hurt?
– do I need to do anything about any relationship as a result of this hurt?
– have I grown as a person in any way as a result of this experience?
– have there been any benefits to anyone or anything else?
– could I use this experience to benefit me in the future?

If you are unable to answer these questions for yourself at the moment, try doing one or more of the following:

– reading about similar experiences
– watching relevant TV programmes and films
– talking with people who have been through the same or similar experiences
– talking to people who were involved in the hurt.

You can't be brave if you have only had wonderful things happen to you.

MARY TYLER MOORE

(Bonus) Step 6 – Channelling

Our aim: *to find a constructive outlet for using the positive benefits and learning from our emotional wound.*

At this stage I am on very solid ground. I must be one of the world's greatest experts on Channelling. I first started practising it as a toddler and have now built a successful career out of it!

But although I now feel I have learned to manage my Channelling skills and can use them constructively, for most of my life I used them in a way which, although admittedly of some benefit to others, almost destroyed me.

My Own Experience of Self-destructive and Constructive Channelling

As the eldest child in a family with an alcoholic mother and a father who was working abroad for much of the time, I quickly learned to bury my own unhealed pain under a mound of 'big sister' bossy protectiveness. This was extended to many other 'brothers and sisters' when I reached the harsh world of children's homes. In my confused and lonely early teens I became intent on saving the world with constant prayer and good conduct. By 17 I had developed another channelling dream. I would shatter the consciences of the rich and powerful with unforgettable documentary drama. Although by then I knew for certain I was no saint, I was nevertheless totally unaware that my motivation was fuelled in the main by my own secret mound of emotional pain and turmoil.

By my 21st year, financial need had forced me to compromise my dream. Instead I became a stalwart social worker in one of the seediest, most run-down areas of Great Britain. A few years (and many unhealed hurts) later my own emotional banks burst. A short spell in the anti-therapeutic atmosphere of a large mental institution set me back to the familiar comfort of Channelling once again. I absorbed myself in my self-appointed role as rescuer of abused and battered 'children' of all ages, while I dampened my own emotional pain with barbiturates and alcohol.

And so the story of my life limped on in a similar fashion for many years until the inevitable burn-out and breakdown interrupted the pattern. But, even after my own lengthy and thorough emotional healing, my Channelling habit stuck. It was well and truly programmed into my personality and it helped me earn a highly soul-satisfying living. I didn't want to lose it, so I learned how to manage it and transform it into a constructive force for both me and the people I wanted to help.

Recently I have been very grateful for my channelling skills. Indeed, I give them much of the credit for enabling me to recover my strength so quickly after my daughter's death. Setting up Laura's Foundation (to enable other young people to pursue their life-dream) was my automatic, almost instant response to this deeply traumatic wound. But thankfully, by this time I had become super-aware of the dangers of moving too fast through the healing process. First, I knew that under this extreme stress I had jumped automatically into 'Bonus land', and secondly I knew that Channelling was one of my greatest strengths and would undoubtedly play a major role in my recovery.

I therefore accepted my need for my Channelling plan, but I took great care that it did not interfere with my need to work through the first five essential Emotional Healing steps. So, although I sowed the seeds of Laura's Foundation only days after her death and continued to feed and water them from time to time, I brought others in to tend its pilot work. A formal launch date was not set until over a year later when I could feel confident that I would have recovered enough emotional and physical strength.

From this latest personal experience I have learned something new about Channelling. It has taught me that, although it is a Bonus step in the healing process, *as long as it does not interfere with the completion of the essential stages* we can (if we are so inclined) start making plans for it very soon after our hurt. Keeping the fledgling Foundation at our sides has been comforting and inspirational for myself and many others as we have journeyed down our dark, seemingly endless tunnel of intense grief. Without this new wisdom I might well have been advising you to put all thoughts of Channelling well away until you were fully healed. (Are you noticing my Perspective in Action?!)

Hopefully you have also spotted another important piece of wisdom on the subject, which I hope my own story has illustrated. If someone is using Channelling without self-insight, and believes that their motivation to do 'good works' is *purely* altruistic, the therapeutic benefit to themselves, and to others, will be severely limited. *In the hands of a still deeply wounded person, Channelling is ultimately counter-productive.*

And now a final warning before we get into this next bit of action! Channelling should never be used to press either your own, or others', *guilt buttons.* If you have judged that this is not an appropriate step for you, don't look over your shoulder in shame and envy at others enjoying its powers. Remind yourself that it is *not* essential to emotional healing *and there are also many other ways of making a contribution to the world.* However, before you dismiss it completely as an option for sometime in the future, please read the following section because you may be surprised to learn about some of the less obvious ways you can use its healing energy.

Channelling in Action

Use the following list of symptoms to help you do a spot-check on your emotional wound. If it reveals that you may need to backtrack a little, you may still gain some benefit and motivation from making a few channelling plans.

Symptoms which may indicate that wounds are still not adequately healed:

- thoughts about the hurt interfering with your concentration
- disturbed sleep or eating patterns
- unusual levels of forgetfulness/apathy/obsession/fearfulness/worry
- bursts of feeling which surface unexpectedly and perhaps inappropriately

– anxiety reactions to people or situations which remind you of the event
– new or increased phobic behaviour
– physical tension
– health problems which could be psychosomatic in origin.

Review the learning you noted when working on Perspective. Use this list of examples to jog your mind into action.

Examples of Constructive Channelling

- raising awareness by talking about the subject regularly
- befriending a lonely elderly neighbour
- volunteer work for a relevant charity
- working for an organization whose mission is sympathetic to your cause
- fundraising
- joining, or starting, a pressure group
- giving talks on your experience on how to handle or prevent the hurt
- suggesting, or joining in, radio phone-ins on the subject
- writing letters of complaint
- writing a letter to your MP or Ombudsman
- writing an article, pamphlet or book on the subject
- political campaigning for a party who promises a change of relevant policy
- becoming a local councillor or MP
- becoming a magistrate
- becoming a school governor
- composing a song or piece of music on the subject
- planting bulbs or trees
- erecting a memorial bench or sculpture in a public place
- coaching young people in relevant skills
- teaching first aid
- teaching stress management
- teaching adults to read and write
- giving clothes and bric-a-brac to a charity shop
- mentoring new or junior colleagues
- writing a play, television or film script

- writing your autobiography
- peer counselling
- couple counselling
- AIDS counselling
- adopting or fostering a needy child
- teaching others about emotional healing!

Other ideas will include doing your own Brainstorm; choosing an idea which seems both feasible and appealing to you; doing a Mind Map to help you explore a path towards your channelling goal.

Write yourself a detailed Action Plan, using the following headings as a guide:

1. my ideal long-term goal (e.g. 1–10 years)
2. the level of achievement I regard as an acceptable compromise
3. my goal for six months
4. my goal for next week
5. my sources of regular support
6. the method I will use to keep a check on my emotional health
7. the signs that I am using Channelling successfully
8. the strategies I will use to cope with setbacks
9. what I will do if I am unable to achieve my goal.

Show your Action Plan to a good friend (it could be the person who helped you through the Comfort stage) and ask them to check whether it sounds reasonable. You don't necessarily have to abide by their judgement, but sometimes someone from outside the situation can spot more easily when we are not being realistic or fair to ourselves.

(Bonus) Step 7 – Forgiveness

Our aim: *to shake hands (physically or metaphorically) with the person or persons who perpetrated our hurt, and move forward into a new relationship free of malice, grudges and ill-will.*

This final step is only appropriate for hurts where we can clearly identify a person or a number of people who are responsible or partly responsible for inflicting our hurt. Unfortunately it is *not available* for some, such as those caused by:

- an act of fate
  - a truly freak accident where a random number of causative factors happened to meet in an unpredictable way
- a random quirk of nature
  - an unexpected storm or disabling gene
- a vast mass of people
  - a hurt inflicted by a sudden surge of rebellion or anarchy on the part of such a large group of people that it is almost impossible to apportion blame or responsibility because the factors involved were so general and may even have built up over a number of generations.

Even if you *can* identify the perpetrator or perpetrators of your hurt, it may not be possible for several other reasons which will become obvious as I discuss this step.

How I wish forgiveness was as easy as so many well-meaning people seem to make it out. I often see it heralded in self-development articles, books and courses as the cardinal key to happiness, psychological health and satisfying relationships, as well as eternal salvation! Such evangelical calls to the dizzy and sometimes unattainable heights of forgiveness are not only fodder for irrational guilt, they often inhibit sound emotional healing and render us, and others, more vulnerable to further hurt. In our impatience (or ignorance) we may reach too quickly for this final stage and skip crucial steps of our essential healing, and also repeatedly blind ourselves to otherwise obvious risks.

Here are some examples which I hope make my point. Although they are extreme, I can assure you that variations on these themes are all too familiar to the ears of agony aunts, counsellors and social workers.

- the ever-pardoning duped divorcée who limps from one relationship to another and ends up cynical and lonely
- the overly trusting friend who resorts to blind drunkenness to lift his spirits after a few too many betrayals
- the martyr mother whose self-esteem reaches rock-bottom because she finds it hard to keep internally smiling through the constant drip of put-downs which she valiantly soaks up from her insensitive family
- the too-willing victim of school bullying who refuses to betray his 'apologetic' abusers and is punished himself for causing disruption
- the 'nice boss' who eventually gets the sack for his staff's repeated abuse of deadlines or company policy
- the battered partner who is instantly seduced by appealing, 'sorry' eyes and ends up with one beating too many
- the 45-year-old 'child' of demanding and manipulative parents whose own children suffer as a result of her repeated absences and stress-induced illnesses

- the eternally 'easy-touch' parent who is shattered when the teacher rings to say their teenager has been found stealing from the staff room lockers.

The kind of Forgiveness we are seeking is different. It *grows from a feeling of compassion which **sometimes** emerges spontaneously, genuinely and freely* as a result of completing each and every one of the essential steps of Emotional Healing. The growth of such a feeling cannot be forced. Attempts to do so only lead to 'phony' and shallow forgiveness, which may fool the world but rarely fools the donor who often feels inwardly fraudulent and despondent.

But although Forgiveness cannot be forced, it can be nurtured along its natural path a little more speedily. Two factors play a part in this:

a) an insight gained by the hurt person which indicates that the perpetrator was not acting maliciously, and may not even have been conscious of the impact of their hurtful behaviour or attitude

b) a genuine change of heart and sincere apology on the part of the person who gave the hurt.

Through your work on Perspective you will already have nurtured the first. (If not, return to page 83 for a refresher course!) And before you start into action, please remember that however hard you try you may never succeed in getting some people even to admit that they have hurt you, let alone apologize for having done so. So never allow yourself to forget that *although Forgiveness is a commendable and satisfying goal to reach, it sometimes poses an unrealistic and unreasonable challenge – and no one, but no one, should ever feel guilty if they cannot reach it, even in the whole course of a lifetime.*

Forgiveness in Action

Give some consideration to the possible negative consequences of trying to prompt the person who hurt you into an explanation or apology. For example:

– the person may be too old/young/confused/preoccupied/stressed/self-centred to be able to either understand, recall or discuss the incident and you could end up feeling frustrated. Or they could suffer needlessly and you would be left feeling guilty or sad for having 'forced the issue'
– the person may not be enough in control of their emotions for a rational or safe conversation to take place, and you could end up getting hurt again.

In a meeting or in a letter, spell out assertively to the person whom you hold responsible (or partly responsible):

a) the feelings you experienced in reaction to the hurt
b) the impact it has had on you and your life.

If you do this well (and with calmness and courage), your chances of receiving a satisfactory explanation or an apology will be greatly enhanced. Use these tips as a guide.

How to Start Forgiveness Discussions
- If you have arranged a face-to face talk with the person concerned, script out and practise what you are going to say to open the conversation. This will help you to keep control of your emotions.
- Don't beat about the bush, come to the point as quickly as you can.
- Indicate that you are no longer speaking from a highly charged emotional state (this will reduce the risk of them leaping to the defensive).
- If appropriate, empathize with what they must be feeling about bringing up the subject (if this is too hard to do, you may not be ready for Forgiveness).

- Don't accuse the other person of *making* you feel anything – (i.e. 'I felt …' not 'You made me feel …').
- Quote your sources (e.g. Don't say '*Someone* told me …', name the person).
- Don't attribute motives to them. Instead, ask them directly for an explanation if you think it will help you to forgive.
- Acknowledge any responsibility you may have.
- Speak in a calm, factual, even tone (be careful not to use one which has an accusatory or whining touch to it – it's very easy to do, unless we consciously control our voice!).
- Finish on a positive note, indicating what you (and perhaps they) might have to gain if they give you the apology or explanation which you are hoping for.

Examples

To a colleague who 'stole' a contract:

Terry, last week when I found out that you had gone behind my back and approached one of my customers and taken an order, I was very hurt and angry. I apologize for going hysterical in the office in front of everyone. I've calmed down now, but I still don't trust you. I would appreciate some time to talk it over with you. Perhaps then we'll find a way of working together without any hidden feelings or suspicions getting in the way.

To a parent who forbade contact with certain friends:

I've recently been doing a course on parenting which involved looking at my own childhood. I know what I am going to say might seem a bit trivial, and you may not even remember the incident, but the feelings have lingered on and on. My recollection of it is that when I was 13 I brought some friends home, and you refused to let them stay for tea, and later said that they were not my type and I should not invite them again. I was shocked and angry, but I didn't know how to tell you. I just sulked and became determined to see them whatever you said (and I did!). When I talked it through with Mary I found I was crying, so it obviously did hurt me a lot. I feel much better now, but realize that it may have been the reason why, even now, I don't talk to you much about my friends. Do you remember the incident?

To a friend who has slept with your partner:
Adam, I know that I am raking up dirt from the past which we've all been trying to forget, but the fact is I'm not really over it yet. You know I was shocked beyond belief to hear from Sarah that you and she had been to bed together while I was away in June. At the time I couldn't face talking to you – perhaps I should have done but, to be honest, I was afraid that if we did meet I might have killed you. But I've done a lot of thinking, talking and yelling since then. I think I am well on the way to putting it behind me. Sarah assures me that you feel devastated about the whole thing, and that it just happened because you were both drunk and we'd had a row before I left.

I'm not sure if you and I could ever be friends again, but I thought if I could hear your side of the story directly from you, there might be a better chance of us wiping the slate clean – and at the very least, it might help me to trust Sarah a bit more.

After your discussion or exchange of letters, if you want the relationship to continue it is a good idea to re-negotiate it at this point to try to prevent yourself getting hurt again. State clearly what your expectations are, and what would happen if they were not met. For example:

I would like us to continue being friends on the condition that we are completely open and honest with each other, but if I find out that you have gone behind my back again, this time I will report you to management and our friendship will be over.

If the person who hurt you is dead or not able to be contacted, you can still take some action which might help Forgiveness to develop and grow. In the course of dramatherapy sessions I often use techniques to bring the person 'back to life' so that a Forgiveness conversation can take place. A few of these can be used if you are working on your own, but only if you have worked through all the other essential Healing steps and your wound is no longer raw. (If in doubt, ask a good friend to be with you, or consult a counsellor). You may need to give one of these techniques a try before you'll be convinced that it works – I certainly did!

- Write a letter to the person concerned; take a few minutes to think yourself into their 'best shoes' (i.e. recall the positive aspects of their personality) and then write a letter back to yourself as though you were them.
- Use creative visualization to have an imaginary meeting with the person. This will only work well if you have taken yourself into a deeply relaxed state and spent 5 to 10 minutes recalling some of their best qualities.
- Use two chairs and move between each as you have a conversation. It sometimes helps to put a photo on the chair, but obviously doing this is more likely to bring up strong emotion.
- Write a poem, song or short story which spells out your forgiveness (if it sounds contrived and is obviously not coming straight from your heart, you will know that you are in 'phony forgiveness land').
- Plant a flower, tree or shrub as a token of your absolution.

You cannot prevent the birds of sadness from flying over your head, but you can prevent them from nesting in your hair.

CHINESE PROVERB

DOG ROSE

THE PET SHOP

Key 3

Harness Your Habits

– with Positive Strategies for Runaway Feelings

This is essentially a self-help practical work section which I have designed to help you regain control of feelings which have become so intense, or so frequent, that they are getting in the way of you doing what you want to do, or being the kind of person you'd like to be. I suggest that you give it a quick read-through first and then decide which parts are a priority for you to focus on first. You can then re-read these and do the exercises which I suggest. I am hoping that you will also use this section as a handy supportive reference tool which will be here to help you should you need a boost to your emotional confidence at any time in the future.

First you will find a simple quick-fix strategy to help you instantly apply the brakes to your unwanted emotional responses and encourage you to take positive action instead of continuing to remain helplessly dependent on their mercies.

There then follows information on eight specific feelings, intended to be a guide on how to break the habits underpinning these runaway feelings so that you will be permanently more in control. I have used the same basic structure for discussion and self-help work on each emotion, to be used as a framework for dealing with any other troublesome emotion with which you may be having difficulty. (You can do this either on your own, or in a small self-help group.)

The feelings which I have selected are:

Guilt
Shame
Anger
Fear
Jealousy
Envy
Apathy
Unbridled Love

I have not included sadness and disappointment in this section because I hope you agree that these have been well enough covered in the section on 'The Emotional Healing Strategy' (*page 55*). You could, however, use the same format to look at these or any other feelings.

I have organized the chapters under the following headings:

Its protective message – as I have said earlier, all emotions have been designed as survival aids. When we are experiencing difficulties with certain emotions it is hard to remember this fact. It helps to start our positive action by reminding ourselves that it is not the feeling that in itself is 'bad', it is simply that it is not being well managed and has been allowed to get out of control.

Its related emotions – under this heading I have named other emotions which are similar in nature to the one being discussed, because much of the material would be applicable with only a small amount of modification. I have also named emotions which are often experienced in tandem or are felt as a result of the mismanagement of the particular feeling.

Its common hurtful habits – I have selected three ways in which, if mismanaged, an emotion can lead to habitual patterns of behaviour which are usually self-sabotaging or can hurt others. I have illustrated each of these with a couple of examples of the habits in action. You'll see that they can affect an enormously wide range of people, from all ages and all classes.

Discussion – here I briefly describe some interesting general aspects of each emotion (why problems are particularly prevalent today and whether the feeling can, when better controlled, be useful to us). It does not matter whether you find yourself either agreeing or disagreeing with some of the points I make. Either way I hope you will find them a useful starting point for you to do some more thinking and research around the subject.

If you are working on your own, you could take a pause from your work on this book and read another one on the subject, or talk to friends and gather their thoughts to compare with mine and your own.

If you were working on this programme in a self-help group, you could use this section to stimulate a chat on the general issues around the emotion. This would be a useful, safe 'warm-up' to the more personal work in the later exercises.

Childhood factors which may have programmed your brain with unhelpful and inappropriate responses – here I list some of the common root causes of problems with this particular emotion. Again, it is intended to be a starting point to your own analysis. It is very important to know how our childhood experiences have affected our 'bad habits'. If we know how our brains have been programmed to respond in relation to each emotion, we can prepare specific strategies to counteract the negative habits. For example, if we know that one of the reasons why we feel so guilty is that our father had such unrealistic expectations of us, we can be on our guard against a) unrealistic goal-setting formulae/demanding too much of ourselves and b) over-reacting with guilt or anger when someone else makes challenging demands of us.

Hopefully this section could also be a useful guide and trigger for discussion and thought among people in a parenting role.

Adult habits that can keep unhelpful responses active – here I've listed some of the everyday habits for which we ourselves are responsible, and which can sabotage our chances of keeping control of the given emotion. Please adapt and add to my list from your own experience.

Tips for better management – ways which I and other people have used to help us handle this emotion in a better way. Again, please add your own ideas and ignore those you find irrelevant. Hopefully the act of reading my tips may stimulate your own ideas, especially if you are working in a group.

BALM exercise – which I suggest you do immediately and then again each time you have trouble with the emotion. With entrenched habits we may often need to repeat this kind of personal development work several times before our brains get the message that we mean business!

Balm is a mnemonic: the four letters of the word will remind you of the four areas of work which I suggest you do on each emotion, and the best order in which to tackle them. Under each heading you will find questions to answer and tasks to undertake.

1. **B**enefit – to motivate you to do the work, you will find it helpful first to remind yourself of the 'pay-offs' you can expect as a result.
2. **A**ttitude – suggested ways to change the unhelpful beliefs which you have programmed into your subconscious mind about this emotion.
3. **L**ifestyle – suggestions for reviewing your lifestyle and making changes so that you will be less vulnerable to your 'bad habits'.
4. **M**anagement – to help you clarify which specific strategies you need to have 'at the ready' should you experience trouble with that emotion again.

Reminder! – finally, I have finished the section on each emotion with a short reminder of the benefits to your confidence once you can enjoy better control of it. You might want to photocopy some of these and pin them up around the house or at work.

ACHE into Action

A quick-fix strategy for runaway feelings

Here is a simple strategy you can use when you (or others whom know you well) first begin to notice that your emotions are hurting you or someone else. ACHE is a mnemonic of its key words, so its stages can be remembered very easily. The idea is that you are giving the thinking part of your emotional brain an instant action plan so that it can more easily take over control.

The ACHE mnemonic
A is for ACCEPT
C is for CONTROL
H is for HARNESS
E is for ENJOY

Accept

The first step in taking control is to accept:

a) *that we are feeling the feeling* – even if we are ashamed of our emotional state or would rather not be feeling this way. Remember that denial is a common defence which we use to shield us from troublesome feelings. It can be useful only as a temporary emotional block, as when we have many practical problems to sort out first and cannot deal with our feelings immediately.

So, say to yourself: 'I accept that I am feeling … '

b) *our responsibility for our own emotional experience* – even if we would like to blame someone or something else for making us feel the feelings. Remember that projecting responsibility is another common response to troublesome feelings. This defence can be spotted very easily in our language. For example, we might find ourselves saying:

'You are making me angry'

'You make me feel really guilty when you ... '

So, accept your responsibility by saying instead:

'I am getting angry ... '

'I feel guilty when you ... '

c) *our responsibility for controlling our action responses* – even if we currently think that they are out of our control. Remember that it is common to fool ourselves that we had no alternative but to behave in a certain way in response to a feeling. Again, we can hear ourselves saying:

'I couldn't help it, I was too much in love'

'It just happened – I was feeling so ... '

'The weather made me so lazy – I just couldn't be bothered'

'He frightened me so much that I didn't say a word'

So, say to yourself:

'I accept that I can choose how to act in response to my feeling of ... '

Control

The next step is to take control over your physiological responses. For many emotions this will mean using a strategy to induce a state of calm in yourself. For emotions such as apathy, however, it will of course mean that you have to energize your system.

So do your deep breathing or meditation, or get exercising!

Harness

This step involves harnessing the habit which encouraged your feeling to get out of control.

So, turn to the section on the relevant emotion and plan some action!

Enjoy

This step is easy but often forgotten! It involves reminding yourself that you will soon be able to take pleasure again in the emotional side of you.

So, tell yourself that feeling something is far, far preferable to feeling nothing, and that now you are taking control of your feeling it is no longer a danger, it can only enrich your experience of life.

GUILT

((Protective Message))

'You have, or currently are, disrespecting one of your inherited values or one of the standards you have set for yourself.'

Related Emotions ☲

Guilt is often experienced together with Shame, but there are distinct differences (*see page 117*).

Common Hurtful Habits ☡

Obsessive worrying about whether we should have achieved more, even when we are obviously successful:

> *John, an overseas buyer, negotiates a good (but fair) bargain for his company but stops himself from enjoying the thrill of his success by worrying about whether this 'proves' that he ought to have done better with the deal he did yesterday.*
>
> *Lorna, a student who has until now always achieved C grades, finally gets a B – but instead of feeling pleased she can't stop thinking about the A grade she might have got if only she hadn't gone to that party last Saturday.*

Slipping into self-punitive and self-destructive behaviours and lifestyle:

> *Marianne is on a diet. She has a bad back and has to lose some weight. She finds herself taking one forbidden biscuit with her coffee. She feels mortified with guilt and ends up 'comfort-eating' her way through the rest of the packet. She finishes the whole packet.*
>
> *For some years Bob has been unhappy in his marriage. He doesn't understand why and feels very guilty about the fantasies he has about other women. He tries to make it up to his wife by buying her and the children extravagant gifts which he can ill-afford. His debts secretly mount. One evening, tempted by the comforting 'shoulder' of a female colleague, he is unfaithful. An affair begins which he immediately nurtures with even more borrowed cash. He is disgusted by his own behaviour and begins to 'drown his sorrows' on a habitual basis.*

Sabotaging our moments of happiness and tranquillity by continual musings over what we haven't achieved, or others' less fortunate circumstances:

> *Lucy, a young mother who treats herself to a well deserved weekend break and ruins its benefit by worrying about the pile of ironing she didn't manage to do before leaving her Mum, whom she hasn't visited for months, and the children who are left at home with their 'poor' father.*
>
> *Joe and his wife are having a rare blissful evening at home with their feet up in front of the television and a delicious takeaway. A friend, whose marriage has just broken up, rings and wants Joe to go out for a pint. Joe declines the invitation but ruins the rest of his evening by 'beating himself up' with guilt and shame for being so selfish.*

I am sure you will have no difficulty in adding some more examples of your own under each of these headings, because I have focused on just three of the bad habits that out-of-control guilt can foster!

❨ Discussion ❩

Why is guilt such a common problem today?

There is no simple answer, and therefore unfortunately no simple, fast solutions. A few of the general factors which I suspect are contributing to what many therapists see as an epidemic of guilt are:

- our world is changing and developing too fast for most human beings to keep up the pace – isn't it true that no sooner have we learned a skill or acquired some knowledge than it is out of date? The rate at which new methods, data, research, policies and ideas are now produced in all fields means that it would be hard for a genius to keep on top of the latest theory and practice. This is true not just for the skills we may need to do our work (such as the best word processing programme to use for writing books!) but also our personal skills (such as parenting or the 'in' way to dress or ask for a date). This means that we are often aware that we are not doing as well as we could be doing – even though our 'doing' is good enough!

- sophisticated mass media and advertising techniques are now continually drip-feeding our subconscious minds with unrealistic standards and arresting images of 'perfect' people in perfect homes leading perfect family lives supported by a perfect bank balance! Two minutes of flipping through the pages of a glossy magazine are enough to make the average person feel guilty about at least one area of their life.

- moral boundaries have become infinitely flexible, as many of our traditional guardians are losing their own moral power (church leaders, politicians, teachers, parents, etc.). Our daily lives are peppered with unsettling dilemmas, such as:
  - if we have children, should we or should we not work full-time?; should we allow the kids to watch what they want on TV or should we play censor?; should we call them 'kids' or is that a put-down?; should we have sex before marriage or should we remain virgins?; if we earn above a certain figure (what figure?) or win the lottery, should we give 5 per cent or 10 per cent or even nothing to charity?; when we have a day off should we spend 85 per cent of it with our partner or should we reserve 50 per cent of our precious time for ourselves? Should we use our savings to help our ailing father jump the medical queues, or should we let him risk dying in a democratic queue?

Previous generations had many more hard-and-fast rules and authoritative rule-makers to guide them. Nowadays we've grown wily and suspicious about 'incontrovertible' evidence and statistics, while at the same time there seem to be fewer people whom we can trust to tell us what is *undoubtedly* the *right* thing to do. The TV and other media are constantly confronting us with opposing research and views from erudite experts (and alternative parent-figures) on so many issues. This liberalizing of our cultural codes means that we are constantly faced with the loneliness and stress of making difficult decisions on our own, in the full knowledge (with its accompanying guilt) that we could be doing the 'wrong thing'.

In such an unstable moral climate, a certain level of guilt is both understandable and inevitable. So (unless we want to burden ourselves with even more of this difficult emotion!), our aim in managing guilt has to be to reach 'good-enough' standards, and certainly not perfection. But even this goal is not that easy for many of us. I know that I'm still struggling. The people who know me well also know that guilt still has a very prominent place in my Achilles heel. Fortunately I am married to someone who shares this problem, and by playfully pressing each other's 'hottest buttons' we can at least have some fun amidst our angst.

Of course, there's more to beating the guilt habit than just a bit of gentle teasing from knowing loved ones. The first step must be to gain *a thorough understanding of what makes us so vulnerable* to developing and maintaining the habit. You can start by becoming more aware of the influence of your childhood.

Childhood Factors ✚

Here are some of the factors in childhood which may have programmed your brain with unhelpful and inappropriate guilt responses:

- Did you have an overly critical/authoritarian/punishing/ unforgiving parent figure?
- Were you being taught by overly strict or pushy or unrealistic teachers?
- Did you have a parent or other much-loved person who was severely or continually sick or unhappy at an age when you may have thought you were to blame (i.e. most of your childhood!)?

- Were you directly (or indirectly) compared unfavourably to any of your brothers, sisters, cousins, neighbours children, your friends or any other 'Superchild'?
- Were you surrounded by role-models who had little control over their own guilt buttons?
- Did you practise and fervently believe in a religion which had set standards so high that only a saint could live up to them in this life?
- Did you often feel you had to keep your bad behaviour or failures a secret for fear of being hurt or rejected?
- Were you continually fed with stories and images of people who are worse off than yourself? (e.g. most post-war Jewish children were haunted by the Holocaust, and many grew up feeling guilty for being alive)

Note down any other childhood experiences which may have had a significant influence on your ability to control guilt.

Adult Habits □□

The following are some common examples which can keep unhelpful guilt responses active. They may be consciously or unconsciously practised. Do any sound familiar to you?

- choosing people to live and/or work with who are similar to our judgemental parent figures from childhood
- setting ourselves up for failure by selecting work and other goals which are beyond the scope of our potential (or the potential of any living being!)
- on achieving a success, immediately comparing it to someone else's greater achievement or effort
- judging our current achievements against the better standards we may have reached in the past (e.g. putting ourselves down because we do not have the figure, face or mental agility we had when we were 20, even though we look great and are still functioning well)
- not living up to our own standards

- fantasizing about hurting others or doing wrong
- ruminating too long on our wrong-doings and mistakes
- unnecessarily sharing our faults and mistakes with others.

Add to my list from your own experience, and note down some current examples of your own 'guilt habits'.

Tips for Better Management ☆

Each time you begin to feel your guilt surfacing, instead of getting depressed or self-punitive, take some positive action. Read the following list of tips and then do the BALM exercise (*opposite*) to give you some ideas of what to do.

- Maintain a clear set of values which are continually reviewed and updated (e.g. be able to list instantly your own 10 'commandments' in hierarchical order).
- Know which inherited values you still have programmed into your subconscious which are likely to trigger guilt responses, and be ready to counteract their power with a prepared strategy.
- Keep your assertiveness skills in good working order so that you can defend your own values when they are challenged (even by those in authority).
- Keep a realistic view of your potential by doing 'post-mortem' assessments after each of your successes and failures, and by asking for objective feedback from people whom you respect.
- Check that you are giving yourself a fair chance of achieving your potential and goals by having adequate skills, knowledge and energy.
- Make action plans to use the learning from mistakes.
- Respond quickly with amends or apologies each time you have hurt someone.
- Take adequate support from people who respect your values, enjoy your achievements and stay with you through your failures.

BALM □□□

Benefits

What do you stand to gain from taking more control over your guilt?:

I'll make quicker decisions and be able to concentrate better on my work/studies/sport.

My legs won't go to jelly the moment someone starts to criticize me, or I see a police car approaching.

I'll have a better relationship with Mum if I am visiting by choice and not out of guilt.

I'll be able to enjoy my success.

What price could you ultimately pay for holding on to your guilt habits?:

Poor health and perhaps a few years of my life.

A bitter old age full of regrets.

My resentment might begin to eat away at my love for the children.

What treat are you going to give yourself for working on your guilt habit for the next month?:

A trip to the cinema.

A drink or meal out.

A new book or CD.

Attitudes

What inherited beliefs do you have programmed into your brain which keep you tied to your guilt habit, and to whom do these beliefs really belong?:

'Mistakes are inexcusable' (my Maths teacher).

'Marriage should last a lifetime' (Mum/church/John).

'You should not fancy someone much older or younger than you' (society).

'Women should always put their children first, husband second and themselves third' (grandmother, father and media images).

Which affirmations will you use to counteract these 'foreign' attitudes the moment they spring into your mind?:

I am the judge and jury of my chosen moral standards.

I have a right to make mistakes.

I am a responsible person.

I am good-enough.

Choose at least one encouraging relevant quote or saying to put in a prominent place:

> *As you commit beyond a shadow of a doubt that you'll never allow the behaviour to occur again, you have a right to let go of the guilt. Guilt has served its purpose.*
>
> ANTHONY ROBBINS

> *Feelings of guilt drive people towards sacrificing themselves completely to a cause or to their fellow beings.*
>
> MELANIE KLEIN

> *Life's too short to stuff a mushroom.*
>
> SHIRLEY CONRAN

Choose one more way to reinforce your new attitude in your subconscious mind:

I will carry a photo of … . to remind me.

I will use … . as a symbol and take it with me to work.

Each day I will play … . music/song.

Lifestyle

What changes will you make in your lifestyle to ensure that you will be less troubled by guilt?:

Go to bed earlier so I am not always tired and bad-tempered in the mornings.

Only work late one night a week.

Walk to the station instead of taking the car.

Review my finances and decide what savings I can make so I can afford a reasonable donation to the charities of my choice in the coming year.

Set aside one weekend a month to devote to my relationship with … .

Management

What are the chief warning signals in your body, mind and behaviour which you can use to warn you that your guilt is escalating?:

Persistent tension headache.

Immobilizing myself by worrying about all the things I haven't done.

Saying 'sorry' three times when once would have sufficed.

What strategies could you use to calm your guilt response instantly?:

Do some meditation (*see page 42*).

Use re-framing to change worrying thoughts into positive ones (*see page 37*).

What action will you take to reduce the general level of guilt you are currently harbouring?:

Write a thank-you note to Richard, and apologize to Jill for snapping at her in the meeting (tomorrow).

Buy Luke a new CD for forgetting to bring back the one he lent me (within the next few days).

Pop in to see Sophie as I've heard she's off sick (within one week).

Sort and decorate the back bedroom (within six months).

Whom could you turn to for honest feedback and support when you suspect irrational guilt is starting to escalate again?:

Joseph at work.

My brother.

Someone from my networking group or professional association.

SHAME

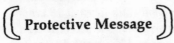

'Your self-esteem and well-being are too dependent on other people's approval.'

Related Emotions

Embarrassment, inferiority, shyness and loneliness are often by-products of shame. It is also often confused with guilt, but there are distinct differences even though they are often experienced in tandem.

Common Hurtful Habits

Hiding ourselves or parts of ourselves:

> *Penny often bites her tongue instead of contradicting an obviously stupid suggestion at meetings because she's frightened to be seen as argumentative.*
>
> *David buys a 'boring' middle-class car instead of the 'flash number' he'd much rather have because he's ashamed of his working-class background.*

Developing a 'false-self' through constantly trying to be someone we are not in order to please others or sink unnoticeably into the background:

> *George is, by nature, an introvert and good with his hands. He struggles to becomes a famous academic doctor instead of quietly running his own small garage of classic cars, which has*

always been his dream. His father would be ashamed to have a mere mechanic for a son.

Jill is a quietly spoken housewife with a part-time job as a shop assistant. She has long since forgotten how brilliant she was at school and that she was once leader of her gang. She was, however, the ugly duckling of her family and when at 18 years her first boyfriend asked her to marry him she accepted even though she knew she didn't love him and had wanted to go to university. Her friends and family were obviously very surprised that she had made such an impressive 'catch' and could not understand her hesitation about accepting his offer. For 25 years, she has lived (apparently happily) in this man's shadow. At 18 she was mildly ashamed of her appearance, but by the age of 43 she was thoroughly ashamed of being Jill.

Becoming ego-centric in our thinking:

Richard goes to a party and is unable to relax and enjoy himself because he keeps on wondering if other people in the corner are really discussing the weather or the election or the girl with green eyes. He worries that they must instead be talking about him.

Each time Brenda walks into a changing room, she 'knows' that all eyes immediately start focusing on her awful stomach or untidy hair, big nose or tatty bra. She cannot concentrate on looking at the clothes she wants and usually leaves the shop in despair.

Discussion

The root cause of shame is low self-esteem. The feeling is triggered by any experience which makes us believe that we, as people, are not measuring up to a 'good-enough' standard in the eyes of the world outside us. Unlike guilt, we do not necessarily have to do or think anything wrong, before we can have this feeling. We can have it just by being the person we are – or think we are. We can feel shameful about our basic genetic inheritance such as our nose, feet, race, height or even gender.

We can only feel shame as a result of someone else's judgement. There has to be a set of grades against which we measure ourselves and these have to be given to us (however long ago and however subtly) by others. We are not born with a concept of a 'good-enough' nose or skin colour. We acquire these standards from our experience in the world, and through responding to value judgements (particularly from our key parent-figures) about our worth.

Like guilt, shame may have been invented by 'Mother Nature' as a form of social glue. It helps societies gel together as a cohesive, strong group because it reinforces their shared values (e.g. about what constitutes beauty, classiness or bad taste) and it keeps the people who don't measure up to these values quietly sitting at the bottom of the social pile. For example, in a society that puts a high value on courage, the people who prefer a safe, uneventful life might well be ashamed of their cowardly avoidance of risks. This feeling would make them less likely to challenge their brave leaders, however aggressively and unjustly these leaders are wielding their personal power. Similarly, in a culture which puts a high value on blond hair, blue eyes and protruding ribs, the brown-eyed cuddly brunettes may watch patiently as the fair-haired sticks flirt with their males. Their feelings of shame about their physical imperfections render them the easiest of prey and make them much more willing to make do with their paragon's rejects.

Shame is both an uncomfortable emotion and a very frightening one, because it is so bound up with social isolation. Not only are we inclined to hide when we feel it, others reject us and ignore us when they recognize that we are someone who doesn't match up to the required standard. In many societies this aspect of shame is consciously cultivated by the people in power as a way of ensuring obedience. They make feeling this feeling an integral part of the punishment which they give to those who do not comply with their rules. Some obvious examples of this use of shame would be:

– forcing children to admit their low marks in front of the class, stand in a corner or even wear 'dunce's caps'

- stripping people of titles and medals
- administering public beatings and hangings

In some societies, lower-order members are made continually to wear 'uniforms' which help feed their shame and therefore make them more amenable to taking servile roles (e.g. maids' aprons, or the yellow stars for Jews ordered by Hitler during the Nazi regime). Alternatively, they may keep them confined to geographical areas which have acquired low status. Apartheid in South Africa was an obvious national example, but a more mundane one (which many of my clients can recall) is keeping the most superior room in the house strictly for adults.

Is Shame Intrinsically Bad?

Although I have been dwelling on the negative uses of shame, let's not forget that it can sometimes have a very positive effect. It can humble the arrogant and make the insensitive more aware. Gandhi was an example of a leader who used the feeling in a positive way. He shamed the British into reviewing their colonial power. Third-world charities also use this technique. They justifiably use shame to make us dig deeper into our pockets to relieve poverty and distress which we might otherwise ignore.

Such positive uses of shame are, in my experience, the exception rather than the rule. If you're reading this it is likely that you are only too aware of how it suffocates potential, eats away at confidence and contaminates even well-deserved happiness. If you belong to a post-assertiveness generation, maybe you will need even less convincing of its destructive power. It is likely that you view shame as a highly demeaning emotion to have. I am finding that this new awareness can make it even more difficult for young people to admit they need to do something about the feeling. They are so ashamed of being ashamed, they frequently deny their pain.

Unfortunately, even when we have the courage to face this potentially pernicious emotion, most people find it particularly difficult to shift and take control. This is largely because its roots are usually deeply embedded in our personal identity. If you are particularly vulnerable to feeling this emotion, please don't give up too soon. It may take a couple of years, not months, to break the entrenched habits, but once you have you will literally feel like a new person.

Childhood Factors 🏥

Here are some of the factors in childhood which may have programmed your brain with unhelpful and inappropriate shame responses:

- Did you receive less than adequate love from one or more parent figures? Or did you perceive that you were less loved than you needed? (e.g. Mum or Dad preferring a brother or sister or being emotionally too crippled themselves to show enough affection)
- Were you rejected or abandoned by a parent? Or did you think you were rejected or had been abandoned because perhaps you were too young to understand? (e.g. about divorce, death or adoption)
- Were you born into a class or race or family which was not held in high esteem by your society, or your influential role-models or peers (e.g. being poor, black or Jewish; having a bankrupt or unemployed father, or an alcoholic mother)
- Were you constantly being compared unfavourably with others? (e.g. with the swot brother at university or Mrs Jones' little princess next door)
- Did you have an imperfect or socially disapproved of body (e.g. having a physical disability such as poor eyesight or hearing/a crooked nose)
- Were you teased excessively or ridiculed (e.g. being called 'four-eyes'/'fatty'/'ginger'/'cauliflower ears', etc.)
- Did you constantly achieve below-average academic results at school?
- Were you excessively criticized even when you felt you were trying your best?

- Were you told, or given the strong impression, that your best wasn't good enough?
- Were you subjected to any kind of emotional, physical or sexual abuse?

Note down any other childhood experiences which may have had a significant influence on your ability to control your shame.

Adult Habits ☐☐

The following are some common examples which can keep unhelpful shame responses active. They may be consciously or unconsciously practised. Do any sound familiar to you?

- constantly, and unnecessarily, comparing ourselves unfa-vourably with other people
- giving ourselves put-downs in front of others and inviting unwanted criticism
- developing a 'clown' personality (e.g. making ourselves a figure of fun through non-stop jokes against ourselves, and 'acting silly' too often; becoming the 'fall guy or gal' for other people's humour)
- behaving in ways which confirm to ourselves and the world that we are shameful (e.g. becoming dirty and unkempt in our appearance, homes and offices; drinking or eating too much; having affairs; petty crimes)
- working or socializing too much with people who are judged by us, them and society in general to be of a supe-rior breed, and with whom we cannot find any common ground on which to break down the barriers (e.g. living in an area that is too 'posh' for our income bracket; working with people who have a trail of letters after their name and insist on talking in jargon we haven't a hope of understanding; shopping in stores designed to attract people 20 years younger or 30 kilos lighter)

- not protecting ourselves from abuse (e.g. allowing others to shame us in front of friends; allowing lovers to have sex with us when we are not inclined; bosses to underpay us or heap unfair workloads on us)
- blocking our own success (e.g. not putting ourselves forward for the promotion we know we deserve; holding back from asking desired people for a date; not sharing our views and ideas at meetings).

Add to my list from your own experience, and note down some specific examples of your own 'shame habits'.

Tips for Better Management ☆

Each time you begin to feel your shame surfacing, instead of hiding away or keeping quiet, take some positive action. Read the following list of tips and then do the BALM exercise (*page 124*) to give you some ideas of what to do.

- Always heal your emotional hurts and abuses, even the small ones and half-forgotten ones. (Learn the Emotional Healing Strategy off by heart!)
- Regularly feed your self-esteem with self-nurturing, good deeds and achievements.
- Avoid unnecessary self put-downs. For example: 'This dress is too small for me' (not 'I'm too fat for this dress').
- If you have to be self-critical, use self-respectful language, avoid exaggeration and focus on your behaviour, not YOU as a person. For example: 'I have a tendency to talk rather quietly' (not 'I know no one can ever hear me. I'm such a mouse.') 'I made a mistake. I took the wrong turning. I apologize for being late' (not 'I'm such an idiot, I never understand directions, I've got a brain like a sieve – not like you. You always remember everything.')
- Play on your strengths and don't put the focus on your weaknesses:

– Sandra, spending two hours shopping for clothes to highlight her good hair colour rather than giving herself a depressing weekend, spending most of it trying to find the miracle garment to hide her slightly protruding stomach

– David, spending his precious holidays trying to be the DIY person he'll never be, instead of using his wonderful nurturing, fun qualities to play with the children or earn some pin money by being a coach for the local youth club

- Give yourself adequate treats and pampering during stressful times, especially if no one else is likely to do so.
- Refrain from indulging in self-destructive behaviour (e.g. smoking or drinking too much when you know you'd prefer to be someone who didn't do this).
- Taking adequate support from people who enjoy your strengths and accept your weaknesses, and not disappointing yourself by turning to people who constantly want to change you.
- Constantly check that you are being yourself as often as you possibly can be, and that you are not unnecessarily playing a role in order to be the person others may expect or need you to be.
- Keep an eye on your goals and ensure that they are in line with what you want for yourself (at least in the long term).
- Never draw attention to habits which reveal your shame or shyness (e.g. blushing or a nervous tic).

BALM □□□

Benefits

What do you stand to gain from taking control of your shame?:

I will be healthier because I will feel free to buy the nutritious food I like/go to the gym when I want to go.

I'll have better self-esteem and more confidence.

I'll stop blushing.

What price could you ultimately pay for holding on to your shame habits?:

I will not be as successful at work as I want to be (and deserve to be).

I won't attract the kind of person I want for a partner.

I'll just get fatter/thinner/more dependent on alcohol or drugs.

What treat are you going to give yourself for working on your shame habits?:

A weekend away on my own because that's what I'd like.

An item of clothing made (to fit ME) by a dressmaker or tailor.

An aromatherapy session.

Attitudes

What attitudes have been programmed into your brain and are blocking you from breaking the shame habit, and to whom do these really belong?:

'Pride comes before a fall' (my cynical head teacher).

'Men should always take the lead' (father).

'Black people are inferior people' (racists).

'Only thin people are beautiful' (the fashion and slimming industries).

'Men with money (or muscles!) are the "real men"' (workaholic and 'gymaholic' friends).

Which affirmations will you use to counteract these 'foreign' attitudes?:

I am proud of who I am and my achievements.

I enjoy being 'second mate' to Gillian, and I do an excellent job.

I am proud of being black.

I am beautiful.

I feel masculine and I am masculine.

Choose at least one encouraging relevant quote or saying to pin up in a prominent place:

> *In itself, shame is not bad ... Healthy shame is the psychological foundation of humility ... toxic shame is the core of most forms of emotional illness.*

JOHN BRADSHAW

He that has no shame hath no conscience.

PROVERB

It's our light not our darkness which frightens us ... playing small does not serve the world ... we are all meant to shine as children do ... as we let our own light shine we unconsciously give other people permission to do the same.

NELSON MANDELA
– AT HIS INAUGURAL ADDRESS, 1994

Choose at least one more way to reinforce your new attitude into your subconscious mind:

Treat myself to a very good portrait photo and display the result!

Wear a new outfit which I have bought for myself

Keep on a small card in my briefcase a list of my six main strengths and six of my major successes in life.

Lifestyle

What changes will you make in your lifestyle to ensure that you will be less troubled by shame?:

Stop pretending that I like having lunch on my own, and join the group or go to the pub.

Every Monday go to the self-help group for people who share my problem.

Set aside one weekend a month when I give priority to pure self-indulgence.

Make sure that I put something on the agenda for each project meeting.

Management

What are the chief warning signals in your body, mind and behaviour that your shame is around?:

I start lowering my voice and people have to ask me to speak up.

I make excuses about going out at weekends.

I begin to worry again that people are looking at me or talking about me behind my back.

I start blushing.

What strategies could you use to help you defeat your shame responses?:

Use positive self-talk about myself (*see page 37*).

Do a self-esteem building programme.

Prepare assertive scripts to help me speak out (*see pages 44 and 76*).

Make yourself a step-by-step action plan to reduce your sense of shame and build your self-esteem over the next six months:

Ring June and 'confess' my feelings about my ... (within the next 24 hours).

Tell Julie how hurt I felt when she attacked me personally in the project meeting (within one week).

Enrol on an evening course in Italian (within six months).

Whom will you ask to support you and check on the progress of your action plan?

_____ .
_____ .
_____ .

REMINDER!
Shame under our control gives us more confidence to be the person we are.

ANGER

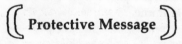

(**Protective Message**)

'There is a threat to your well-being or the well-being of someone or something you care about.'

Related Emotions

Various names are used to describe the various degrees of
anger, ranging from frustration and irritability through to fury
and rage. Depression can be caused by anger being turned in
on oneself. Apathy is often the result of denied chronic anger
(*see page 171*).

Common Hurtful Habits

Bursts of irritability or rage at the wrong time, in the wrong
place and to the wrong people or objects:

> *Brian publicly sulks throughout the special night out at his
> favourite restaurant which his partner Sue has prepared for his
> birthday. He is inwardly angry with her but also with himself.
> The previous week, Sue forgot to book their holiday and he has
> not yet told her how disappointed he really is. He knows this
> pattern is now common in his marriage (just as it has been in
> every other of his relationships with women), but he doesn't
> seem to be able to do anything about it. Soon there will be a
> major bust-up over the most minor detail in their everyday lives.*
>
> *Lorraine is a working mother with two children of six and
> eight years old. She is continually struggling with the frustra-
> tion and guilt which she has given herself through her hectic*

lifestyle. She has had a frustrating day at work and is feeling particularly bad because she knows that she allowed her boss to manipulate her into taking home some extra work. She arrives home and the children run up to her and give her a big hug. She immediately feels better. Five minutes later she can hear herself screaming with rage at them because they've started to quarrel about who should bring in the biscuit tin to her. She feels devastated by her lack of control and starts to cry. The children go very quiet – they are confused and inwardly very upset by 'the awful thing' they have done to Mummy.

Swallowing the tension and rendering ourselves speechless, motionless, depressed and sick:

Gael (yes, me!), while in her thirties developed severe arthritic symptoms in her hands and chronic sinusitis as a result of a build-up of physical tension over the previous six months. During this period she had been inwardly raging after hearing the devastating news that she had been constantly deceived by her first husband throughout their seven-year marriage. 'For the sake of the children' she had maintained a smiling face to the outside world and struggled to be understanding and loving towards her husband.

Jane is 15 years old. She does not consider herself to be pretty and has been overweight for the last few years since the onset of puberty. Unlike most of her group at school she has never had a boyfriend. In contrast, her mother is highly attractive and maintains her 'youthful figure' by keeping herself constantly on the latest diet plan. Jane, instead of screaming angrily at her mother when she 'nags' or teases her about her weight or her 'scruffy' appearance', binges behind her back.

Crying victim's tears and inviting more abuse:

Hannah is the manager of a team of telephone sales operators working in a rapidly declining market. During an appraisal session when her management style is unfairly blamed for her team's poor performance, she finds herself crying instead of defending herself and her team. Her boss then launches into an attack on her personality, saying she is over-sensitive and too timid a person to survive in the new competitive markets.

Ten-year-old Paul misses two easy goal chances in a row. The coach makes fun of him and Paul, instead of defending himself by becoming justifiably angry (hard to do when you're 10 years old and your bully is the teacher!), becomes upset. In the changing rooms later, he overhears a group from the team talking and laughing about him because they noticed the tears in his eyes.

ꝯ Discussion ꝯ

It is now hard to believe that at the start of the 1990s I was told by my publishers that there would not be a big enough market for a book on anger. I don't dispute that at the time this was wise advice, but now, less than a decade later, only a hermit with giant blinkers and ear plugs could deny widespread public interest in the subject. It's no longer just therapists like me with privileged ears to personal secrets and pain who are concerned. Politicians, teachers, doctors, sports coaches, business managers, film-makers and parents are now all crying out for better anger management. Last night I noticed that even the newscaster on our main news ended his broadcast by reminding the nation to keep their cool during any frustration they might meet on their travels over the public holiday.

But it is not just fear of being the subject of others' out-of-control anger that is prompting interest. I find that more and more people are now willing to admit that they themselves are having trouble controlling their own mounting frustration.

Why Has Anger Become Such a Problem for So Many of Us?

Apart from the social and economic causes (such as too many people chasing too few resources) which are often discussed, I would suggest there are a number of other trends which have fanned the flames of general concern:

- The right to be treated with respect and justice has increasingly become an expectation for the mass of people all over the world.
- The freedom to express our feelings, and to assert ourselves when these expectations are not met, is increasingly seen to be a human right, in both our personal and public lives.
- Very few people have had the opportunity to learn, either through formal teaching, role-models or practise, safe constructive ways to manage their anger.

Perhaps the reason why I first became so aware of these particular trends in their early stages is that they are exactly the ones which I experienced in a very personal way, more than 20 years ago. After my 'nervous breakdown' in my twenties, a spell of nurturing psychotherapy helped me become aware of how unjust my deal in life had been. I emerged knowing that I had a right to feel the feelings I was currently experiencing. The sense of emotional liberation I felt was fine as far as my feelings of loss and sadness were concerned. It was relatively easy (and safe) to give myself the space and permission to whinge, moan and cry. But when my anger inevitably began to emerge I found myself totally out of my depth. The therapy had sent me swimming in an unfamiliar (and dangerous) sea of feeling – without instructions and without a life raft!

Of course I didn't have this awareness at the time. It took a further stream of emotional and physical crises and years of crippling guilt and self-disdain before I began to realize what was at the heart of my problem: I hadn't yet learned and practised the skills which would help me to keep my anger under my control. From the age of toddler tantrums I had developed a habit of keeping this emotion locked away. No one had time to teach me how to manage my own early outbursts; they were much too busy and too preoccupied with their own personal frustrations which I saw (and felt!) being expressed in an uncontrolled and violent manner.

Putting right this deficit in my own social education was, of course, not easy. To my knowledge there were no Anger

Management courses or books around at that time. But, little by little, I did find other ways to get some help. Fortunately I came across the new technique of Assertiveness Training and many of the new alternative therapies which began to grow in the late 1970s in Britain. I threw myself into as many of these as my meagre bank balance could afford. A few proved to be well worth the investment, but very many seemed to make matters much worse. I would watch others rant and rave at cushions while my own inner rage just turned more and more sour.

After a few years I began to do what many have done before: I started to teach what I still needed to learn! Interestingly, I can now see that it was these experiments in my own anger courses that personally helped me the most. Preaching what I was trying so hard to practise reinforced both my motivation and my determination to stick to my new habits.

Childhood Factors ✚

Here are examples of factors in childhood which may have programmed you with unhelpful and inappropriate anger responses:

- Did your parents either deny or 'swallow' their anger?
- Were you emotionally or physically hurt by a parent or other significant individual who often lost control?
- Were you blamed for making others become angry and lose their control?
- Were your own early experiments at expressing anger unfairly disapproved of or punished? (e.g. parents with an over-authoritarian approach to temper tantrums)
- Did you receive encouragement to feel anger and express it in the 'wrong' way? (e.g. 'Don't take it from him, give him a crack he won't forget' or 'She's no right to do that to you, but don't let her see you're upset, just find a way to get you're own back when she's not looking!')
- Did you hurt others with your anger but find yourself subsequently denied guidance on how to express your feeling more safely?

- Was your mind fed with an over-dose of images of destructive violent anger through the media? (e.g. violent videos, magazines and songs)
- Were you continually confronted with examples of 'saintly martyrs' who never lost their temper or felt even a twinge of anger? (e.g. were you, through your religion, given the impression that you could jump the queue to heaven by being placid in the face of abuse?!)

Note down any other childhood experiences which may have had a significant influence on your ability to manage your anger response.

Adult Habits ▫▫

There follow some common examples of adult habits which can keep unhelpful anger responses active. They may be consciously or unconsciously practised. Do any sound familiar to you?

- playing safe with life and hiding away from, or ignoring experiences, which could trigger off anger
- being with people who have something to gain from our programmed responses (e.g. a boss who gets a kick from goading us into a tantrum; a lover who only loves us when we 'sit back and take it')
- finding a job which pays us for our habit (e.g. pacifying angry customers or 'beating the hell out of' a rioting crowd) and not giving ourselves enough time to switch off from our roles.

Add to my list from your own experience, and note down some current examples of your own 'anger habits'.

Tips for Better Management ☆

- Deal quickly and assertively with minor threats so that there is no build-up of feeling and you have plenty of opportunity to practise handling this feeling in safe situations (*see page 44*).
- Maintain a clear and up-to-date idea about what, by your own standards and for your own needs, is worth getting angry about and what is not.
- Develop a sound knowledge of your own pre-programmed patterns and make a plan to counteract these (e.g. positive self-talk and honest feedback).
- Keep your self-esteem boosted so you are not so vulnerable to wounded pride (probably the most common cause of everyday uncontrolled anger responses).
- Give yourself a balanced lifestyle and nurturing relationships so that you have only tolerable amounts of pressure with which to cope.
- Play a sport or do physical exercise which will allow you to release any pent-up tension.
- Have a constructive channel into which you can direct your justified anger, especially when it has been stimulated by issues which you are powerless to do anything about – either now or ever (e.g. campaigning for improved rights for political prisoners or maltreated animals).
- Regularly check the state of your key relationships, and resolve conflicts and re-negotiate expectations and ground rules as soon as possible.
- Each time an old habit surfaces, take time out to reflect and get feedback on what went wrong and rehearse (if only in your mind) how you can behave differently next time.

BALM ☐☐☐

Benefits

What do you stand to gain from breaking your bad anger habits?:

I'll be less tense and have fewer headaches/backaches/stomach upsets, etc.

People won't be so afraid to give me criticism, and so I'll be able to improve my ...

I won't feel so guilty about my parenting and can relax more with the children.

What price could you ultimately pay for holding on to your bad anger habits?:

My children will learn these habits and suffer as a consequence.

I could hurt someone if I were to blow my fuse eventually.

I could lose my job.

What treat are you going to give yourself for working on your anger habits in the next month?:

A new tie.

A day out at the seaside.

A contribution to my holiday fund.

Attitudes

What inherited attitudes do you have still programmed in your brain which are keeping you tied to your anger habit, and to whom do these beliefs really belong?:

'Anger is dangerous and just gets you into trouble' (my violent friends at school).

'If you give in to anger you'll go crazy' (Mum).

'Turning the other cheek is what the truly great and saintly do' (church).

Which affirmations will you use to counteract these 'foreign' attitudes?:

I have a right to express my anger in a safe and constructive manner.

Swallowed anger could make me depressed and send me crazy; well-managed anger keeps me emotionally healthy and gives me energy.

Using the power of my anger to protect my own and others' rights is both courageous and sensible.

Choose one or two relevant and encouraging quotes to pin up:

> *Only a person with no feelings and no awareness would not feel the smoulder of anger, even rage, deep inside at times.*
>
> **ANNE WILSON SHEAF**

> *Anyone can become angry – that's easy. But to be angry with the right person, to the right degree, at the right time, for the right purpose, and in the right way – that's not easy.*
>
> **ARISTOTLE**

Choose at least one more way to reinforce your new attitudes:
  Play the music of …
  Put up a picture of …
  Put my stress ball on my desk.

Lifestyle

What changes will you make in your lifestyle to ensure that you will become less frustrated and irritated, or angry?:
  Stop seeing …
  Eat more regular meals.
  Say 'no' to uninvited guests.
  Say 'no' to ridiculous demands at work.

Management

Which are the chief early warning signals in your body, mind or behaviour which tell you that you are getting angry?:
  Body: tapping foot; tense jaw
  Mind: dwelling on what has happened even when I am supposed to be working.
  Behaviour: higher-pitched voice; getting obsessional about tidiness.
What strategies could you use to control your feelings?:
  Deep breathing exercises.

Daily Yoga.

Don't Get Too Boiling strategy (*see page 46*).

Improve my assertiveness (*see page 44*).

Re-read a good book or listen again to a good tape on anger management.

What step-by-step action will you take over the next six months to take better control of your anger?:

Write out two affirmations and read them before going to sleep (within the next 24 hours).

Suggest a lunch meeting with …. to talk about our relationship problems (next week).

Do an assertiveness training course (within six months).

Whom could you ask to support you and give you honest feedback while you are working towards improving your anger habits?:

_____.

_____.

_____.

REMINDER!
Anger under our control gives us more confidence to stand up for our own and other's rights.

FEAR

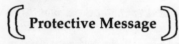

(Protective Message)

'There is a threat to your welfare which you are not yet capable of handling.'

Related Emotions

Anxiety and worry.

Common Hurtful Habits

Restricting our opportunities by playing safe with our lives and avoiding new experiences and those which have in the past been hurtful:

> *Jack has been hurt several times as a result of having personal relationships with colleagues. He made a rule for himself never to date another person in the office. A year later he starts to fall in love with a new colleague and knows that they are very well matched, and his feelings are returned. He refuses her suggestion of a date because he cannot handle his fear of another let-down.*
>
> *Janet wins two air tickets for the kind of holiday she has always dreamed of, but pretends she cannot go. The sad reality is that she has turned them down because she is afraid of flying.*

Brooding and ruminating about minor details and concerns as a way of avoiding a major threat or concern:

Pat is inwardly terrified of developing the hereditary disease which has disabled so many of her family in the past. She denies this fear to anyone who brings up the subject, but is constantly fretting about the fat content of every meal she and her family eat.

Bill, a senior manager, is deeply worried that he has lost control of his team and that they no longer look up to him with respect. He is much too fearful to confront this major problem, and in fact makes the atmosphere worse by becoming obsessively controlling over their record-keeping and expense claims.

Becoming bored and boring, and finding our relationships sliding into stale, predictable patterns:

Angela has always had a fear of loneliness and, to avoid facing its threat, spends all her social time mixing with a staid set of friends and acquaintances she has known most of her life, in spite of the fact that she knows they no longer stimulate or interest her. As a result she has lost her own innate adventurous spark and has become equally sedate and boring.

Albert and Marion married at 18 years old. Both realized very quickly that they were not happy even though they cared deeply for each other. Ten years on into the marriage, neither has yet plucked up the courage to speak to the other about their unhappiness for fear of hurting the other and 'rocking the boat' to the point of capsize. Instead they prop up their life together with a predictable stream of rituals and routines. They always celebrate each other's birthday with elaborate surprise parties; Valentine's day is spent at the same glamorous restaurant; they take their holidays together on the same romantic isolated island where they spent their honeymoon; and they always spend Sundays going for a country walk after their lunch together. To others they appear to be the perfect couple; only Albert and Marion know how empty and lonely they now feel in each other's company.

☾ Discussion ☽

Fear is one of nature's greatest gifts. It has been designed to help us survive, thrive and play our part in driving the human race forward. Babies and toddlers are drawn towards its thrills. They have no fear of fear. They ask for frights again and again. Much of their spontaneous early play (remember peek-a-boo in the pram?!) centres around this emotion. By playing with fear, children test out their potential and test out the world.

Fear helps us to gauge when our instinctively-driven explorations of life are reaching a point which we are not ready to handle. When it is working well, it guides our instinctive drive forward at a secure, steady pace. We all need a certain amount of anxiety to fuel our motivation and quest for learning and development. But what that 'certain amount' is, for each unique person in the infinitely variable challenges that life presents, even Mother Nature cannot predict precisely.

So our fear response is in essence a self-help alarm and braking system. It is designed to let us know when we have pushed ourselves too fast into the unknown, or when we have gambled with too high a risk. When the 'danger' is perceived, it has the power to freeze our system and pump us full of additional strengthening chemicals to enable us to fight or flee the threat.

Unfortunately, its braking system is proving to be too crude to meet the demands most of us make of it – even in our everyday lives when we are not being severely threatened. The pressurized lifestyles we give ourselves, and our overcrowded communities, push our fear button too fast and too furiously. The sophisticated knowledge we now have about ourselves and the world do not appear to have helped us in this respect. We are even more aware than previous generations of potential threats to our health and welfare. We worry about the food we eat because we now know too much about the harm it could do; we worry about falling in love because we know there are so many factors which could destroy the relationship; we worry about parenting our children because we know how easy it is to make long-lasting mistakes.

As a result, many of us are finding that our fear response is operating quite haphazardly and often seizes up. We can find ourselves being frozen in terror in the face of a minor or imaginary threat, while at other times we may take ridiculously hurtful risks and later wonder why we were so inappropriately fearless. A significant number of people I see have reached a point where their body is in a state of permanent alert. They have completely lost track of what has stimulated their anxiety; they feel permanently nervous, but don't know why.

When you reach this stage it is very hard to keep physiologically in control, and very easy to drift into becoming dependent on substances such as alcohol or tranquillizers. Another danger is the onset of panic attacks. These are highly disabling assaults of anxiety which can surface at any time and in any place, after only the most minor of triggers.

The message I hope I am sending loud and clear is: Take even the most fledgling of butterflies and palpitations seriously. The earlier you start tightening the reins on any troublesome fear habits, the better. As you are committed to working on your personal development, I am assuming you are keen to live an exciting, stimulating life. This is the kind of life that inevitably involves risks and needs to be supported by skilled management of fear.

Childhood Factors ✚

Here are some of the childhood factors which can programme you with unhelpful and inappropriate fear responses:

- having parents who were overly fearful (a mum who was too quick to see the dangerous aspect of every activity and played safe with her own, life or a Dad who was too frightened of change to move from a job which was well beneath his capabilities)
- having parents or teachers who denied your fear ('Don't be silly you can't be frightened of a silly thing like that')

- being surrounded by super-courageous role-models so that you felt ashamed of your own fears and consequently pushed them under (a big sister who was never afraid to make a fool of herself, or a grandfather decked with medals from the war and constantly talked about with reverence by the rest of the family)
- being constantly asked or expected to do things at which you were likely to fail or get hurt by
- being hurt too often (constantly bullied)
- being on the receiving end of a major trauma which was never emotionally healed
- being over-exposed to fear-inducing films, TV shows or videos without the appropriate comfort and reassurance from adults
- being over-protected by parents from even the most minor or natural fears in life ('You don't have to worry, we'll sort it out' or 'You enjoy your childhood while you can')
- not being given adequate information about the biology behind the fear response
- not being given instructions on how to gain physical control of anxiety.

Adult Habits

The following are some common examples which can keep unhelpful fear responses active. They may be consciously or unconsciously practised. Do any sound familiar to you?

- over-loading our life with risks
- thinking negatively (worrying unnecessarily about what is highly unlikely to happen)
- not accepting (or forgetting) that fear is inevitable when we do anything new or difficult and, therefore, not taking steps to control its responses before they control us
- not getting ourselves prepared when we know there is a fair chance that what we are doing may go wrong or fail

- eating foods and drinking drinks which maintain our bodies in an over-stimulated state
- putting courageous people on pedestals and denying their humanity and our own capacity for courage ('He's extraordinary. I could never do what he did, I'd be too scared')
- constantly feeding our subconscious with a counter-productive image of ourselves by labelling ourselves as fearful ('I'm a worrier' or 'I'm the world's worst coward')
- not taking adequate time to relax when we are living or working under pressure
- keeping our face screwed up in worry lines
- keeping our muscles in tense positions
- spending too much time with frightened people (friends who are just as shy as we are, or who are equally afraid of spiders)
- not tackling the Big Questions in life ('Why are we here? 'Why do we have to die?' 'Why do awful things happen to good people?') and so denying ourselves a meaningful philosophy and sense of purpose in our lives to ease our natural anxiety.

Tips for Better Management

As soon as you feel your fear beginning to surface, or you suspect that it could surface, keep the following in mind and do the BALM exercise (*see page 144*).

- Keep an eye on your breathing patterns to ensure you are not hyperventilating; regularly practise deep breathing exercises so that when the fear surfaces you will automatically start to take control over your breathing (*see page 35*).
- In stressful situations, make it a habit to do a few stretching exercises every 20 minutes.
- Quiet your racing mind with a simple meditation exercise (keep a Mandala in your desk or handbag, and have a mantra or image ready to use.

- Use affirmations and self-talk to keep you thinking positively (e.g. 'I am in control of my fear'; 'I am calm'; 'This may be difficult but it is not impossible.' *See page 38*).
- Make a contingency plan; note (preferably on paper or by telling a friend) exactly what you will do if you should meet 'the worst case scenario'.
- Remind yourself of a time when you have coped effectively under stress. Replay the scene in your imagination to give your subconscious a clear and vivid picture of the calm or courageous you. Recall the exact physical sensations you experienced, and gently encourage your body to repeat them again.
- Whenever possible, work through the fear in small, manageable, graded steps and monitor and reward yourself after each.
- Practise before going into the real situation, even if you think you should be able to cope (e.g. rehearse your 'speech' out loud or in front of the mirror, or ask a friend to role-play).
- Closely observe experienced, calm people and practise mirroring their body language. Bring your image of them to your mind before entering a difficult situation, and imagine yourself getting advice and encouragement from them. Your body will automatically take up the positions you practised mirroring, and your brain will switch off its alarm.

BALM
□□□
Benefits

What do you stand to gain from taking more control over your fear?:
  I'll have a more exciting life because I'll be able to take more risks and have many more new experiences.
  I'll stand a better chance of promotion.
  I will earn more money and have the home I want.
What price could you ultimately pay for holding on to your fear habits?:

I could become more phobic and lead a very restricted life.

I'll pass my fears on to my children.

I'll die of a heart attack or give myself ulcers.

What treat are you going to give yourself for working on your fear habit for the next month?:

Two tickets for the theatre.

New printer for my office.

Lunch date with ....

Attitudes

What inherited beliefs do you have programmed into your brain which are still keeping you tied to your fear habit, and to whom do these beliefs really belong?:

'The world outside my home is a dangerous place' (my whole family!).

'You can't trust women' (Dad and James and Mark – all divorced and bitter).

'Cross that bridge when you come to it' (society and school).

What re-framed statements and affirmations will you use to counter-act these negative beliefs?:

Sometimes the world presents difficult challenges which test my courage.

The vast majority of women are trustworthy.

I am courageous.

I enjoy challenge.

I am well prepared for all outcomes.

Which relevant quotes or sayings will you use to motivate and boost you?:

Fear is faith that it won't work out.

SISTER MARY TRICKY

Feel the fear and do it anyway.

SUSAN JEFFERS

I felt fear myself more times than I can remember, but I hid it under a mask of boldness. The brave man is not he who does not feel afraid, but he who conquers that fear.

NELSON MANDELA

Anxiety is simply part of the condition of being human. If we were not anxious, we would never create anything.

WILLIAM BARRETT
– BRITISH PROFESSOR OF PHILOSOPHY

What else will you do to reprogramme your mind to think more positively about fear?:

Read (or re-read) the autobiography of ..... (i.e. one of your favourite courageous heroes).

Carry a photo of yourself taken around the time when you achieved .... in spite of ....

Regularly play the music of Beethoven/Shirley Bassey/ Elton John/Pulp ... (i.e. anyone who used music to help them manage challenges positively)

Lifestyle

What changes will you make to your lifestyle to ensure that you remain more in control of your fear?:

I will give myself one hour extra to prepare for ... (a difficult forthcoming event).

Because they can fan my panic, I will not ring or visit .... and .... when I feel frightened or anxious.

I will do deep relaxation or meditation at least once a day for a minimum of 10 minutes.

I will try to ensure that I only take risks with a 20 per cent chance of failure until I have more control of my fear.

Management

Which are your chief personal warning signals that your fear is taking hold?:

In your body: dry mouth; palpitations; headache, etc.

In your mind: loss of concentration; persistent worry; night-mares, etc.

In your behaviour patterns: irritability; a fit of the giggles; phobias, etc.

Which strategies could you use to defeat your self-destructive fear habits?:

Deep breathing exercises (*see page 35*).

Progressive relaxation.

Creative visualization.

Reduce the stimulants in my diet (*see page 36*).

Read a book on beating panic attacks (*see Further Reading list*).

What step-by-step action will you take to help you gain more courage and take control of your fear?:

Tomorrow I will tell Josie about my anxiety attacks before I do presentations (a 5 per cent risk that she'll not want to listen).

By the end of the month I will have applied for a new job and will have made a contingency plan in case I am not successful.

In six months from now I will have at least one new friend-ship which will have taken some courage to initiate.

In a year's time I will be able (in public!) to skate on roller blades/drive/dance the Salsa/sing.

Whom will you ask to give you support while you are tackling your fear habits?

_____.

_____.

_____.

JEALOUSY

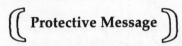

(**Protective Message**)

'Your well-being is very dependent on the love and attention of another person, and your relationship with that person appears to be in jeopardy.'

Related Emotions

Jealousy is usually accompanied by anxiety, and often leads to anger which is usually turned outwards rather than inwards. If the feelings are kept secret, shame usually grows and flourishes. It is frequently confused with envy (*see page 161*), but although the two emotions have distinctively different triggers, they do commonly ride in tandem because some of their root causes are often shared.

Common Hurtful Habits

Sabotaging relationships by constantly checking up on the other person to try and gain reassurance about their love and genuine commitment above all else to your relationship:

Sam has started going out with Nicole, a colleague in a nearby office. She protests to be as keen on him as he is on her, and he has no evidence to the contrary. However, her protestations of love do not stop him from feeling compelled to make excuses to go over to her office, not just to see her but secretly to watch her behaviour with other male colleagues. One evening when she says she is too tired to go out that evening Sam finds himself following her all the way home, and spends a miserable evening sitting in his car watching her door for any sign that she may be going out. He is beginning to hate himself for his 'irrational' behaviour and knows full well (from a previous experience) that it could threaten the relationship. His job could also be in jeopardy, as his boss has already questioned his frequent absences from the office.

Gael (yes me again!) at 14, after her father's recent re-marriage, decides to read her step-mother's diary secretly and finds enough to confirm her suspicion that she is not the preferred child. After leaving home she chooses a series of relationships with married men, of whom she knows (in her head if not her heart) that their wives or children will always have priority. These relationships and Gael's own self-esteem are also constantly strained by her jealous cross-questioning and secret searching for clues to their preferred love.

Inability to share the other person and being overly demanding of their time and emotional energy:

Emma is jealous of her best friend Susan's other friends. Susan has recently moved to Emma's town, and the two women immediately strike up a deep friendship. Susan, however, keeps in regular contact with the friends she had in her last town. She often goes back to visit them at weekends, and occasionally they come to stay with her. Each time this happens Emma provokes a row or sulks. Whenever Susan confronts her with her jealousy, she denies it flatly and often feigns disinterest in her activities with her old friends, although she cannot contain the odd bitchy remark. The situation comes to crisis point when Susan announces that she is going on holiday with one of her old friends. Emma cannot contain her jealousy and confronts her. She is deeply hurt to hear Susan say 'Much as I like you, I would never go on holiday with you. You're much too draining; I'd never get space for myself.' These were almost the same words that Emma's ex-boyfriend used when he broke up with her.

Since the birth of their 18-month-old baby, Rick and Maria have quarrelled constantly. The rows always centre around what Rick calls Maria's 'obsession' with the baby. Maria is finding herself freezing Rick out of her heart. She cannot tolerate his jealousy of what she considers her 'normal mother love'. She accuses him of immaturity, and blames his mother for doting on him. The latter remark often throws Rick into a frightening rage. Maria is relieved when he goes out to the pub to calm himself down. She settles down to an evening (the first of many to come) of worrying about what life will be like when their second child, due in two months' time, is born.

Taking actions which have the intention of making the other person jealous – in an attempt to prove how dependent they are on you, and/or trick yourself into thinking you can survive quite happily without them or their love:

Anne has been married to Jonathan for 18 years. She is beginning to suspect that he has the wandering eye for a younger woman, even though she has every reason to believe he is genuinely devoted to her. Her neighbour's husband recently ran off with their au pair and she knows Jonathan is surrounded by attractive young women at his work. Instead of talking about her jealous fears, she has started to dress provocatively and is secretly planning for a face-lift they can ill-afford. Whenever they go out she openly flirts with other men. Jonathan cannot stand her new embarrassing and demeaning behaviour. They have a massive row and he cannot believe she is jealous of something that has never happened. Later he finds himself thinking enviously of his errant neighbour, and wonders ...!

Adam and Natalie have both been married before. Adam's first wife deserted him and his children for another man. Natalie's marriage came to an amicable end and she is still friends with her ex-husband. Adam is desperately in love with Natalie. He finds his current marriage is much happier than his first, and he is unaware of feeling insecure about its stability. Nevertheless, he keeps on telling Natalie how good a mother his first wife was and often relates stories about their idyllic holidays together. He shows no interest whatsoever in Natalie's friendship with her ex, and will change the subject as soon as he or his life with Natalie is mentioned. Natalie knows that there is some-

*thing wrong between them, but she has not (yet!) realized that
Adam is actually jealous of her ex-partner.*

ℭ Discussion ℈

No wonder jealousy is called the green-eyed monster – it has
the power to cause untold havoc, not just to romantic love but
also to our family and friendship relationships. In addition,
because it is so reviled an emotion and is associated with such
shameful, socially unacceptable behaviour, it devours our self-
esteem.

Interestingly, in the course of history jealousy has not always
been so despised and feared. In fact, for many centuries it was
considered a noble emotion, one which illustrated that a man
(and yes, it was then thought to be a predominantly male emotion) had some honour and deserved self-pride to protect. The
knight who challenged a rival to a duel was not labelled imma-
ture or an overly possessive neurotic, he was applauded and
given hero status. If, in the heat of his passion he took deathly
revenge on either of the offending parties, he would not be
labelled a sick psychopath; he was just as likely to be forgiven
and comforted as punished. Even if he did receive the ultimate
justice, he would go proudly to his death in the full knowledge
that God (who was believed to be a model of jealous wrath)
would look kindly on his ennobled soul.

What Is the Function of Jealousy?

It is likely that jealousy first evolved as yet another emotional
bond which would support the human child through its long
period of dependency. Its original function was primarily to
keep Mum and Dad in a stable relationship throughout their
parenting days. Mother nature, being infamously wily, probably knew that it could be useful in other ways as well. 'She'
might well have seen that it could also help prevent the spread
of sexual disease and provide the sick and the old with a stable
family to care for them. Unfortunately, she didn't have the fore-

sight to see that by the late 20th century it would be so mismanaged that it would become a threat to the children it wanted to protect. They may even suffer more than the adults as a result of its negative powers. It is, after all, one of the prime causes of the breakdown of family ties, and even children suffer directly from many of the stress-related illnesses it can produce.

Is Jealousy Always Bad?

No. Let's not forget that jealousy is not intrinsically an evil emotion. It is a natural self-protective response. It seems to be experienced by most 'normal' people of both genders and in all cultures at some time in the course of their lives. Anyone who has reared pets knows that it is frequently and harmlessly displayed in everyday animal life as well.

Indeed, when jealousy is kept in good control it can even render love more exciting and passionate. It has a well-deserved reputation for being able to revitalize a flagging relationship and prevent it from disintegrating. Unfortunately, today's love relationships, especially the romantic kind, have become so idealized that it is hard to feel satisfied by them. This is perhaps why so many of us are now tempted, both consciously and unconsciously, to 'play with the fire' of jealousy's provocative power. Gentle flirting and teasing games designed to taunt the other person into declaring their love and commitment can most certainly be fun and liven up an otherwise dull party or a quite ordinary night in bed. But equally (as many of you taking an interest in this section will know only too well), games such as these can be agonizingly painful and even dangerous.

Childhood Factors ✚

Here are some of the factors in childhood which may have programmed your brain with unhelpful and inappropriate jealousy responses:

- Did your parents or other influential adults regularly abuse the power of jealousy? (e.g. through unfair teasing and withdrawal of affection just 'for kicks')
- Were you a witness to frightening jealous behaviour between your parents? (e.g. nasty arguments or fights between Mum and Dad over who flirted, or slept, with whom)
- Were you told, or did you get a strong impression, that your own natural, innocent and harmless displays of jealousy were 'evil' and should never be revealed? (e.g. after knocking down a younger sister's sandcastle because she had displaced you on Mum's knee, hearing something like this; 'What a horrible child you are. If you behave like that no one will love you and you'll get locked away one day)
- Did you have a mother or father who continuously gave preference to your brother/sister or their partner/work/ sport or ... over you?
- Were you led by your cultural conditioning to believe that certain kinds of jealous behaviour prove that you are a 'real man' or 'real woman'? (e.g. possessiveness being a revered trait of traditional masculinity and 'turning a blind eye' to infidelity being a trait of the stereotypical dutiful caring wife and mother)
- Were you deserted (or apparently deserted through a premature death or divorce) by a parent figure?
- Did you have a parent figure who was sexually provocative with you but went to bed with someone else? (especially if that person was your mother or your father, so you 'knew' you had no right to feel jealous)

Note down any other childhood experiences which may have had a significant influence on your ability to control your jealousy.

Adult Habits ▢▢

The following are some common examples of adult habits which can keep unhelpful jealousy responses active. They may be consciously or unconsciously practised. Do any sound familiar to you?

- not feeding our relationships with the quality time they merit
- putting too much time, effort and emotional investment into one or two relationships
- burying fledgling fears and suspicions so that they have no hope of being allayed or disputed, and instead fester and turn sour
- spending an above-average amount of time in the company of people who believe in or practise 'free love' or have an overly 'liberal' or cynical view on long-term relationships
- allowing ourself to have an ever-ready listening ear to the tales of woe from 'victims' of disastrous and difficult relationships
- reading too many personal development books or going on too many 'therapy' weekends claiming to have the answers to your quest for the perfect relationship
- not ensuring that we can survive financially without the support of the other person
- not giving ourselves the opportunity to practise leading an independent life from time to time (e.g. going away for a few days on our own or with another friend)
- letting our appearance fall below our own standards
- allowing ourselves to become over-stressed even though we know we are becoming a 'pain' to be with
- letting our self-esteem decline.

Add to this list from your own experience, and note down some current examples of your own 'jealous habits'.

Tips for Better Management ☆

- Set aside a regular time for evaluating and re-evaluating your relationship, and for the rest of the time just enjoy being in it without constantly analysing it.
- If you find yourself indulging in a 'shameful' habit (such as secretly checking up on someone), confess immediately.
- Make a contingency plan for each of your key relationships to use should you get rejected or deserted. This should list specific actions you will take to ensure that you survive and thrive after the event. Don't listen to people who say you are being pessimistic and 'You should cross that bridge when you come to it' – they may not need to be immunized against jealousy.
- Take care to heal extra efficiently if you do get rejected (remember, jealousy is fed by the fear of not being able to recover from loss), before looking for a replacement relationship. And if you haven't done so already, set aside some specific time to heal from deep-seated wounds from the past which are at the root of your bad habits.
- Keep your life outside your key relationships full and satisfying to your self-esteem, so that it can provide a reliable and genuinely motivating distraction to your jealous feelings when they surface (e.g. make sure you have at least one stimulating hobby if work cannot fulfil this role).
- Keep your relationship-making skills well oiled by starting new friendships from time to time, even if you only have time to keep them on a relatively superficial footing. You will be less anxious if they are waiting in the wings should you need or want to develop them (fear of loneliness is a staple food of jealousy).
- Give yourself regular time-out on your own and learn to value and enjoy solitude.
- Don't give yourself an overdose of idealized stories and dramas of perfect love or romanticized tales about jealousy (e.g. stop your subscription to 'True Love Magazine' and hide your CD of *Carmen*!)

- Never kick yourself or denigrate yourself to others for being jealous. Instead, take some positive action and administer some BALM to your anxiety and hurt.

BALM ☐☐☐

Benefits

What do you stand to gain from taking control of your jealousy habits?:

I will stand more chance of keeping my marriage together.

I will get on better with my colleague/sister/father, etc.

I'll need less alcohol to prop me up.

What price could you ultimately pay if you don't kick the bad habits?:

A life of loneliness.

A broken home for my children.

Going down in history as a 'sad case'.

What treat will you give yourself when you have had some success with harnessing your habits?:

A solo holiday.

A night out with …

Attitudes

What disabling information concerning jealousy do you have programmed into your brain, and where did it come from?:

'Jealousy leads to violence' (Dad hitting Mum).

'An ability to practise or condone free love is the sign of a mature, modern woman/man' (the 'sixties' hype).

'Some children are born jealous and you just have to live with it' (Mum).

Which affirmations/self-talk statements will use to counteract these 'foreign' beliefs?:

Well-controlled jealousy does not hurt anyone, including me.

Jealousy is a natural response when the affection from a person we love is transferred to a rival.

What relevant quotes or sayings could you use to help you?:

A little jealousy is not unpleasant ... for it enables people who are not inquisitive to take an interest in the lives of others, or in one other at any rate.

PROUST

Jealousy is not a barometer by which the depth of love can be read. It merely records the degree of the lover's insecurity.

MARGARET MEAD

Jealousy is the fear of losing the thing you love most. It's very normal. Suspicion is the thing that's abnormal.

JERRY HALL

Two people love each other only when they are quite capable of living without each other but choose to live with each other.

M. SCOTT PECK

If you've invested all your self-esteem not inside your own feeling of identity but in possessing the other person, if you lose them, you lose all control.

HANNA SEGAL

Choose at least one more way to reinforce your own beliefs about jealousy:
Read Nancy Friday's book *Jealousy* (*see Further Reading list*).
Keep a special handkerchief (as a reminder of what fate befell Othello!).
Buy, and play, the CD of ....

Lifestyle

What changes will you make to your lifestyle to ensure that you will be less troubled by jealousy?:
I will spend less time with ...
I will stop cross-questioning my partner each time he/she returns from a conference and I will make sure I build in a treat for myself on those weekends.
I'll join the badminton club because I know I am good at ball games and I am likely to meet some outgoing, friendly people.

Management

What are your chief warning signals that a bad jealousy habit has taken hold?:

I take a sneaky look in my partner's briefcase/pockets/diary.

I start making unnecessary phone calls to his/her office.

I find myself gossiping or 'bitching' about ...

I stop looking forward to going out to the pub together.

What strategies can you use to help you defeat your destructive responses?:

Contingency planning.

Affirmations (*see page 38*).

Deep breathing and relaxation (*see page 35*).

Emotional Healing Strategy (*see pages 55–98*).

What is your step-by-step action plan?:

By the end of the week, I'll have talked to ... about my fears.

In a month's time I will have confronted my sister for flirting with ...

By this time next year, I'll arrange a holiday for myself while Joe immerses himself in the World Cup.

Whom will you ask to support you while you are working on your jealousy?:

_____.

_____.

_____.

ENVY

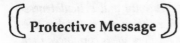

(Protective Message)

'You need something which you do not have.'

Related Emotions

Envy is often confused with jealousy (*see page 149*). It is usually accompanied by feelings of powerlessness, apathy and/or shame.

Common Hurtful Habits

Under-using our own potential and own strengths because we are trying too hard to emulate the qualities, skills or lifestyle of those we envy, or are too choked with resentment even to try to be a success ourselves:

Peter is a shy, gawky 10-year-old who has shown a great aptitude for maths and information technology. His teacher says he is a genius and has the potential to get a first at university and become a leading figure in the world of computers. But the gang of lads who 'lead' his class tease Peter for being a 'boring nerd'. He envies their confidence, competence at sport and casual approach to their school work. He stops bothering so much with his homework and wastes evening after evening lost in the world of his computer games. In this world of fantasy he scores endless goals and constantly saves the universe with heroics that would leave the school gang gasping with admiration and amazement. At 24 Peter graduates with a third-class degree in law (the most popular course of the day but quite unsuited to him). At 43 he is bitterly resentful about his work as a general legal 'dogsbody' for a partnership of smart, brash barristers who are half his age and earn 10 times his salary.

Gael (again!) spends the first half of her adult life living in the shadow of writers and other intellectuals (including her first husband). She envies their creativity and articulateness and also the letters they string after their names. It takes five best-selling books and a belated MA before she is convinced that her talent is equal to those writers and other achievers she had envied. Even now, she sometimes struggles to divert her covetous eyes from lingering with longing on the successes of great novelists, opera stars, Olympic athletes and ...!

Being unable to enjoy (or let others enjoy) our own good fortune and achievements because we are too busy comparing these unfavourably to those of others:

After months of struggle, Jeff has at last reached his sales target. His friends invite him for a celebratory drink. He ruins his evening by surreptitiously trying to find out how long it took each member of the sales team to achieve what he had achieved that day. His friends won't make the same mistake again: in future they'll let Jeff stew alone in his soured success.

Fiona is the oldest member of her slimming club. It has taken a year to shift her middle-age spread and reach her target weight. Instead of feeling pleased with herself and soaking in the compliments on her new figure and better health, she focuses her eyes on the youthful, unlined skin of her fellow weight-watchers. Her family dreads her return from the club each Tuesday night, as it is so boring to listen to her endless envious ramblings. They know tonight will be no different, target or no target. So they all make sure they'll be out when she comes back home.

Looking for holes in enviable people's characters or the elements of unhappiness in their lives, and possibly gossiping with glee about them:

Sandra's older sister Liz was the perfect child and has now become the perfect adult with a perfect lifestyle. She is bright, pretty and always sensitive to others' every need. She has married an equally talented and equally kind man and they thrive in their respective careers while at the same time rearing two adorable, confident children. Although Sandra's own talents and achievements are pallid by comparison, she has always felt equally loved by her parents and by Liz herself. She never feels that Liz is in any way a threat to any of her own relationships or chances in life. She isn't jealous but, deep down, she does feel inferior to her sister and envies her natural aptitudes and the ease with which she has sailed through life. She then hears that Liz's husband is being made redundant. Sandra rushes to see them and inwardly smiles when she sees how Liz has 'gone to pieces'. Every night Sandra rings her fiancé to recount every detail about Liz's ineffectiveness during this crisis. He is shocked to see this side of Sandra's character and begins to wonder if he really knows enough about this woman he was planning to marry.

Greg is a medical student from a poor background who is finding university life a constant financial struggle. His fellow students all appear to have had a better deal in life, and he feels bitter that he cannot afford the cars, clothes and expensive meals that they can. One of the wealthiest of these students, Luke, invites Greg to his parents' holiday home in the south of France for the Easter break. Greg finds that underneath the 'posh' united facade they present to the world, Luke's family is falling to bits. The mother is an alcoholic and the father obviously has no interest in the welfare of anyone but himself and his race horses. In their company, Luke's confident exterior seemed to melt and Greg feels a sense of satisfaction and pleasure as he watches his friend's wimpish behaviour as he is bullied and ridiculed by his arrogant father and selfish mother. On his return to university, Greg spends an evening in the bar entertaining the other students with tales of Luke's family — their hollow 'bourgeois' lifestyle and the drunken dramas of his 'dreadful' parents.

ℚ Discussion ℙ

From the increasing prevalence of books, magazines and newspapers which trade on the misfortunes and misdemeanours of the rich, famous and successful, it seems that Sandra and George are not alone in their self-sabotaging habit. In fact, when I recently visited some friends in the village where we have a farmhouse in southern Spain, there happened to be such a programme on the television. It was explained to me that this was a highly popular magazine programme about famous people, such as film and pop stars and royalty, where all the latest gossip about their scandals and divorces was exposed. (Their successes and achievements were not mentioned!) I found this regular afternoon programme a very sad reflection on our world. Just think of the millions of people passing precious hours of their lives hooked into this envy habit without even the comforting companionship of other gossips?!

Is Envy Always Bad for Us?

Unlike jealousy, envy has no noble history that I know of, but when it is used ethically and with care it can have some good effect. For example, good teachers and coaches consciously use envy to stimulate their pupils to want to achieve their potential and keep them working through the difficult times. They'll point to the success stories in their field ('Wouldn't you too like to see your name on the back of a book in a library?' or 'Wouldn't you too like to be the one standing on a podium with a gold medal around your neck?') Similarly, health educationalists will use the examples of slim, fit individuals living enviable lifestyles to promote their commendable messages, and charities may use role-models who report on their peace of mind and sense of spiritual well-being as a result of giving more freely of their time and money.

Envy is used in this way not because it is intrinsically a good emotion, but because using it this way works. Manipulating people through their desire to have what someone else has got is often a short cut to getting them to do what we want them to do. Every parent knows the tempting power of envy. However hard we may try to use more laudable methods to motivate our children, most of us succumb, from time to time, to using envy to point them (perhaps quite subtly!) in the direction of:

- the new bike that Charlie bought with money he saved
- the shiny hair of the girl next door who always brushes it well
- the three distinctions cousin Jill achieved by only going out at weekends

The intention behind these uses of envy is undoubtedly good, and the end may well be positive. But does that justify the means? Personally I doubt it because it sets up an envy habit which can be so difficult to control. Children who have become dependent on the power of envy to motivate them are easy prey later in life for the less well-intentioned who want to influence their minds and milk their bank balances!

But enough of my sermonizing, let's move on!

Childhood Factors ✚

Here are some examples of factors in childhood which can programme our brains with unhelpful and inappropriate envy responses:

- Did you have parents who constantly looked with longing 'over the garden fence' at their neighbours' superior lawn/new kitchen/latest power shower/newer car or more well-behaved children?!
- Did your mother moan about men's lucky lot in life, or your father moan about women having the better deal?
- Were your brothers or sisters genetically more well endowed than you, or did they seem to have a much easier ride through childhood? (e.g. they didn't have to work the hours you did to pass the same exams; didn't have to straighten their hair; didn't need braces on their teeth, etc.)

- Were you brought up as a member of an underprivileged minority group who felt powerless to achieve what more fortunate members of society could get?
- Were you sent away to boarding school (or any other school) against your will when all your other friends stayed at the local school?
- Did you have to wear your sister's cast-offs when your friends (or, indeed your parents) seemed to spend their weekends shopping for the latest fashion trend?
- Did you spend hours sitting in front of TV ads for better toys, bikes, CDs, holidays than you could ever hope to have?
- Were you brought up in a community where the vast majority of other children had a better quality of life than you?
- Were you a child from a broken home when it seemed that all other children in the world had two loving parents?

Note down any other childhood experiences which may have had a significant influence on your ability to control your envy.

Adult Habits ▢

The following are some common examples of adult habits which can keep unhelpful envy responses active. They may be consciously or unconsciously practised. Do any sound familiar to you?

- exposing our impressionable subconscious minds to too much advertising which uses envy to hook us into buying
- trying to live beyond our financial means
- not accepting our own genetic limitations and continually setting ourselves up for failure by trying to be the kind of person we can never be (e.g. have the singing voice of José Carreras/the football skills of Eric Cantona/the figure of Madonna/the blue eyes of Robert Redford, etc.)
- indulging (too frequently!) in gossip sessions

- asking others for their advice unnecessarily and too often 'Those curtains you chose are so brilliant ... I wish I had your good taste. What colour do you think I ought to ... and do you think I should take that job at ... paint my nails blue, etc.'
- rarely accepting a compliment without retaliating with a superior one ('Oh thanks, but my results were not a patch on yours. What I'd give to have your brains!')
- going shopping regularly with people who have sounder bank balances or better bodies than ourselves
- spending our holidays or weekends window shopping, especially in areas which specialize in luxury items that even an oil baron might think twice about.

Tips for Better Management ☆

- Hold back the mental kicks to your self-esteem. Instead, as the old saying goes, 'count your blessings.' Remind yourself of some of the good breaks life has given you. Complete these two sentences three times each:
  - 'I was lucky when ...'
  - 'I am lucky to have ...'
  - This is not to make you unfairly grateful for a dose of small mercies, but just to switch your brain and its emotional system into a positive mode so you can think more constructively about your envy.
- Check your envious wish against the law of possibilities for you. If it is truly impossible to achieve, immediately counter it with a realistic wish and/or self-appreciative statement (e.g. 'Yes, she was lucky not to have parents like mine ... I cannot be re-born, but I am trying extra hard to give my children the kind of parenting I would have liked').
- If your envious wish is a possibility (however remote), check it against your own core values to see if it really merits the worth you are attributing to it (e.g. 'It's a great yacht but, actually, if I had that kind of money I'd use it to ...' or

'They still seem to be very much in love after 20 years and yes, that is the kind of relationship I would value myself').

- Replace your envy with an achievable goal (e.g. 'She's so lucky not to have a nine-to-five job. In 10 years' time, I intend to be self-employed').

- For a period of a week, ask a good friend to monitor your moans, envious wishes and comparisons of yourself with others. Alternatively, make a record yourself. Just doing the exercise will stop most early in their tracks.

- Keep a list of your core values and your current goals and priorities where you can see them constantly. Review them at least once a year. If you haven't already made such a list, build doing so into your BALM action plan!

- Emotionally heal all your disappointments promptly and thoroughly (*see pages 55–98*).

BALM ☐☐☐

Benefits

What do I stand to gain from beating my envy habits?:
  I will feel less bitter
  I will be more motivated to achieve my own goals
  I'll be happier to put up with …. for the moment
What price could you ultimately pay for not breaking these habits?:
  I will find that I have lived my life according to other people's standards and missed out on what I really wanted, and could have had.
What treat will you give yourself for working on these habits?:
  A session with a good career counsellor.

Attitudes

What unhelpful attitudes do you have programmed into your mind which are supporting these habits, and to whom do they really belong?:
  'Some of us are born lucky and some are not' (folklore).

'It's a man's world' (Mum).

'You can achieve anything you want if you set your mind to it' (overly positive friends!).

Which affirmations or self-talk statements will you use to counteract these 'foreign' beliefs?:

I have just as much chance of getting lucky breaks as anyone else.

Women are changing and they are changing the world!

I can have a happy and successful life in spite of my limitations.

What relevant quotes can you use to help you?:

Envy is a signpost to wanting.

SUSIE ORBACH

Envy and wrath shorten the life.
THE BIBLE – SIRACH (ECCLESIASTICUS)

Choose at least one more way to reinforce your new attitude:

Pin up a list of your own lucky breaks.

Lifestyle

What changes will you make to your lifestyle to ensure that you will be less troubled by envy?:

Spend my holidays in less glamorous locations, so the contrast isn't so great when I get back home!

Make a cup of tea during the adverts on television.

Go to bed earlier so I don't have bags under my eyes.

Management

What are your chief warning signals that envy is controlling you?:

I start listening to Joseph's complaints about me and the veiled comparisons he makes with my predecessor.

I join in the office gossip about the boss.

I start to feel apathetic and adopt a 'why bother?/what's the point?' outlook.

What strategies could you use to defeat these responses?:
   Re-read a book on assertiveness.
   Do some realistic goal-setting.
   Say my affirmations each night.
What is your step-by-step action plan?:
   This week I will record the number of times I feel envious.
   By the end of the month I will have put my business plan to my bank manager.
   By the end of next year I will have started a course in ...
Whom will you ask to support you while you are working on your envy habit?:

_____:
_____:
_____:

APATHY

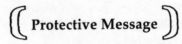

(Protective Message)

'You have lost direction and hope.'

Related Emotions

Underlying apathy, you will often find cynicism, hopelessness, disappointment, boredom or anger.

Common Hurtful Habits

Not bothering to seek out personal development opportunities, and underachieving as a result:

> *Tasmin is 27. She has been in the same clerical job since she left school at 18; during that time has had only one promotion. When she first started she had plans to gain accountancy qualifications through part-time study. After several attempts to get her employers to agree to a day-release course, she lost heart and settled into her repetitive and unchallenging work routine. She no longer even bothers to scan the job advertisements in the papers.*
>
> *Roger is a third-year student on a horticulture course at university. Soon after starting the course he realizes that he isn't interested in the subject, but because he cannot think of an alternative course which he would enjoy, he continues. He has made no attempt to see a career counsellor and has only vague plans for what he will do on leaving university. He says (very unenthusiastically!) that he'll probably just get a labouring job*

in the parks for the summer and see what then turns up. If noth-
ing interesting comes along, he thinks he may go travelling but
he's not sure where or with whom. When asked by a friend if he
has applied for one of the travelling scholarships advertised on
the Department's noticeboard, he says he never gets round to
reading all that kind of 'bumf'.

Becoming unreasonably negative about possible outcomes:

Julian is a 45-year-old father of three. He continually moans
about the education opportunities available to his children. He
has not bothered to vote in the last three elections, and when
challenged about his apathy says that there is 'no point'. He
knows that 'they'll all break their promises anyway.'

Tricia is a 38-year-old divorcée. She has been looking unsuc-
cessfully for a new partner for the last four years. In the first
year she joined many social clubs and made sure that she went
out at least three nights a week. Now she says she has 'got past
caring'. She'd rather not waste her energy on relationships
which would probably end within the month. She is now, by her
own admission, 'addicted to television' and is '... quite happy
to stay that way'.

Allowing others to take the lead and guiding us in a direction
which is neither what we want nor what we need:

Janice has been married for 14 years. When the children were
young and there had been a clash of interests between her
career and her partner's (e.g. when considering a move, or who
should look after a sick child) she always agreed that his work
should take precedence over her own. Over the years she has
become less and less ambitious and has stopped making any
long-term career goals for herself. When her husband has an
opportunity of a post abroad, she agrees to go even though she
knows she cannot get a work visa for herself. Now Janice finds
herself 'resigned' to living in a country which she would never
have chosen to live in, socializing with people with whom she
has nothing in common, and seeing her children only in the

holidays because they have had to be sent to boarding schools back home.

Derek is an award-winning housing architect who, 10 years ago, enthusiastically went into partnership with a friend who specialized in large commercial buildings. Owing to the recession and resulting lack of opportunities for house-building, Derek drifted into an assistant role to his partner on commercial contracts. Now that the construction industry is taking an upturn, Derek is not taking any proactive steps towards getting the kind of housing contracts which would allow him to make use of his creative talents. With a knowing smile, he acknowledges, 'I suppose I have sold out to the easy, safe option. I'm not proud of myself but I can't seem to get around to doing anything about it.'

◖ Discussion ◗

Apathy is an emotion that grows very slowly. It can be insidiously working away for years in our subconscious before we, or anyone else, may even notice its presence. During the time of its build-up its bad habits have much more of a chance of becoming deeply ingrained into our general personality than some of the more 'quick-firing' emotions. We progress, for example, from being:

– someone who feels they 'can't be bothered at the moment' to becoming 'an uncaring person'
– a person who is having 'an off day' to being 'a low-achiever'.

The gradual nature of its growth means that apathy also becomes firmly integrated into lifestyle and friendship patterns. We tend to drift into living in a low-key way, perhaps, for example:

– choosing to live in an unstimulating, 'quiet' environment
– eating bland, ready-prepared foods

– watching sport rather than playing it ourselves
– mixing with people whom we happen to meet rather than actively choosing to befriend, and whom we may 'quite like' but certainly do not excite us.

As this kind of lifestyle may be all around us, it will feel 'normal' and we will feel normal. The people who are living differently will be seen as extraordinary and eccentric – even if they are envied and the dramas of their lives make titillating reading.

Even if someone with a chronic apathy problem is successfully confronted with their emotional state and the harm it is causing them, there is yet another problem to overcome. They very often believe that the fault doesn't lie with them. They are likely to believe firmly that they are victims to external forces which have rendered them apathetic. They will, for example, blame the government for not encouraging them with incentives; their friends for being boring; global warming and pollution for sapping their energy; and shareholders and 'fat cats' for being too greedy and too powerful. If you argue with them, they will typically start by agreeing with you and asking your advice ('Yes, I know I'm a lazy ... what do you think I should do?'). Then, quite frustratingly, they will inevitably find yet another external reason to excuse their inertia ('If I do that, they'd probably sack me/leave me' or 'It might rain/the stockmarket could crash/it might upset everyone.' Eric Berne, founder of Transactional Analysis, describes this kind of repetitive stubborn behaviour as the 'Yes, but ...' Game. He rightly warns that its pattern is particularly difficult to shift, and is almost always a very depressing and non-productive exercise for anyone trying to help. So people who are apathetic soon find their support dwindles to nil, and their paranoia about the world becomes their reality (i.e. however unjust their situation, no one does care and they have been left to 'get on with it' on their own).

Is Apathy Ever Useful?

Certainly a small dose of apathy can help us heal from emotional wounds in the initial stages of our healing. After a major loss, for example, we naturally sink into a state of low energy and may find ourselves unable to be moved emotionally by either good or bad news. Our whole system needs a temporary rest and our feelings of apathy help to ensure that we take sufficient time to recuperate.

This is also true when we have been over-exposed to pressure and are suffering from symptoms of stress. Apathy sucks away our motivation to 'keep going' when it might be clearly dangerous for us to do so. It gives us time to refuel our bodies and re-energize our minds so that we can return to the fray better equipped to solve the problems.

Occasionally apathy can be useful when we are faced with threats which we cannot control. For example, if we are being constantly put down by someone with whom we have to work or someone who holds our job in their hands, and there is no one else who can rise to our defence, allowing ourselves to sink into a state of 'not caring' can save energy and make it easier for us to reconcile ourselves to our unsatisfactory situation.

But of course, like all the self-protective emotions, apathy is designed to be a temporary feeling. If it becomes a 'way of life' we run the risk of becoming seriously depressed and a target for energetic predators and bullies.

Childhood Factors ✛

Factors in your childhood which may have programmed your brain with unhelpful and inappropriate apathetic responses:

- Were you born into a race, nation or social group which has very little political or economic power?
- Do you have a genetic predisposition which causes you to have less stamina and energy than other children? (e.g. overweight, asthma, poor resilience to infection)
- Did you grow up with physical or mental disabilities which meant that life was (and perhaps still is!) a continual 'uphill struggle'?
- Did you have parents who were apathetic most of the time?
- Were you encouraged (or threatened) to go for too many unachievable goals?
- Did you live in an unstimulating and boring environment?
- Were you over-protected and over-nurtured, and not encouraged to do enough things for yourself?
- Were you fed on a non-nutritious or toxic diet?
- Did you get enough fresh air and exercise?
- Were you denied the opportunity of having a wide-enough range of experiences to enable you to find out what, in particular, could 'fire' your own motivation?

- Did you lack encouragement or guidance to set goals or plan a life-dream for yourself?
- Were you left too often or too long in a pram or in front of the television to amuse yourself?

Note down any other childhood experiences which may have had a significant influence on your ability to control your apathy.

Adult Habits

There follow some common examples of adult habits which can keep unhelpful apathy responses active. They may be consciously or unconsciously practised. Do any sound familiar to you?

- not standing up for our rights and allowing others to constantly de-power us
- playing too safe with our lives and not keeping our 'courage muscles' well flexed
- never identifying, or losing sight of, our life-dream
- keeping money too high on our priority list (e.g. overworking at a boring job just for the money and never letting excitement and fun take occasional precedence)
- not spending time with people who can, and will, challenge and confront us
- not maintaining ourselves in peak physical fitness
- being neglectful of our diet.

Tips for Better Management ☆

- Keep your sense of humour well stimulated (spend more time with people who amuse you, go to the pantomime even if you are grown up, etc.).
- Do 10 to 20 minutes' physical exercise at home each morning. (It doesn't have to be too strenuous to work on apathy, and you can energize your mind at the same time by listening to uplifting radio or watching breakfast TV!)

- Keep your creative thinking powers well stimulated (take an evening class; play thinking games, read books on creativity).
- Take your holidays and weekend breaks in new places until you have shaken off your apathy.
- Challenge your cultural programming (learn a new language, read one of the many new fascinating books on world cultures, or just make friends with people from other nationalities).
- Change your diet from time to time (make it a rule to try one new recipe or taste per week).
- Join a group where you will have plenty of opportunity to argue and debate on issues which matter to you with people whose views may be different from your own (join a book or film club).
- Sign up for some voluntary work to help people with a problem, or a cause, which you currently know very little about.

BALM ☐☐☐

Benefits

What do you stand to gain from taking more control over your apathy?:
   I will have more energy.
   I will stop feeling ashamed of myself.
   I will attract new friends.
What price could you ultimately pay for holding on to your apathy?:
   I could become a bitter and regretful grandparent like …
   I will be bypassed for promotion.
   The house will go down in value and we will not be able to have the house of our dreams at a later stage.
What treat are you going to give yourself for working on your apathy habits over the next three months?:
   One whole day doing virtually nothing (but only one!).
   A visit to one of the seven wonders of the world.
   Three new CDs.

Attitudes

What inherited beliefs do you still have programmed into your brain which are feeding your apathy, and to whom do they really belong?:

'There's no point people like us making an effort when you know people like them can just buy their way to the top' (family/class background).

'You never get any thanks, no matter what you do – everyone's out for themselves in this world' (Dad, brother).

'What's the point, you could walk in on Monday morning and find you're redundant' (many people at work, especially since the recession).

What affirmations and positive self-talk can you use to counteract the irrational programming in your brain which is supporting your apathy?:

I am not selfish and insensitive to others' problems, and neither are most people I know.

I enjoy a challenge.

It may be hard but it's not impossible.

Which relevant quotes could you use to boost you?:

The secret of getting ahead is getting started. The secret of getting started is breaking your complex overwhelming tasks into small manageable tasks, and then starting on the first one.

MARK TWAIN

Be the change you want to see in the world.

GANDHI

For me ennui is among the worst evils – I can bear pain better.

MARIE ANTOINETTE

Somebody's boring me. I think it's me.

DYLAN THOMAS

What else can you do to reprogramme your mind with more motivating thoughts?:

Read some autobiographies of people who have succeeded in spite of disabilities.

Write down on a card the names of six people (famous or not) in different fields whom I admire for having achieved success against the odds and keep it, or their photos, pinned up in front of my desk.

Lifestyle

What changes in your lifestyle can you make to ensure that you are less apathetic?:

I'll start each day by doing something which I enjoy (e.g. read a chapter of my novel, or a magazine in the bath for 10 minutes rather than taking a quick shower).

I'll go to bed an hour earlier.

I'll ask … to ring me to check whether I have been to aerobics.

I'll make a 'To do' list for the next day before I leave the office so I can just get started without having to think too hard!

I will make it a rule only to watch TV on three evenings a week and never to turn it on before eight in the evening.

Management

What are your chief warning signals that you are letting yourself slip into a state of apathy?:

Last night's dishes are still there in the morning.

I can't find any clean socks or pants.

I don't complete my 'To do' lists on a regular basis (e.g. three times in a week).

I stop contributing to meetings or start making excuses not to go to them.

I haven't seen a new film for three months.

What strategies can you use to help you overcome your apathy?:

Time-management.

Eat a more energizing diet and cut down on the drink.

Do some creative visualization on my life-dream (*see page 41*).

Do some emotional healing on my disappointment about … (*see pages 55–98*).

Affirmations (*see page 38*).

What step-by-step action will you take to combat your apathy?:

Tomorrow morning I will start a short daily exercise routine before breakfast.

By the end of the month I will have applied for at least two jobs.

By the end of the year I will have a clear life-plan for the next five years, and will have taken the first major step towards achieving my long-term goal.

Whom will you ask to support you in your battle with your apathy habits?:

_____.

_____.

_____.

REMINDER!
Apathy under our control gives us more confidence to use our energy effectively on the activities which really motivate + inspire us.

UNBRIDLED LOVE

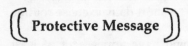

(**Protective Message**)

'You are endangering your own happiness and welfare by caring for others much more than yourself.'

Related Emotions

Uncontrollable pity and compassion. Can also lead to jealousy, guilt and despair.

Common Hurtful Habits

Endangering relationships or the growth of others by smothering them with unnecessary or inappropriate nurturing, concern and displays of love:

Zena is 32 years old and engaged to marry Tony. She has a long history of broken relationships behind her. On the break-up of almost every one she has been accused by her boyfriends of not allowing them enough space to be themselves and lead some kind of independent life outside the relationship. So far, she has 'sat on' her habit with Tony, but now as the wedding approaches she finds herself thinking about him constantly. She feels physically sick whenever he is out driving, and every day finds an excuse to ring him at work to check that he has arrived safely. She has stopped going out with her girlfriends (because she wants to be with Tony or preparing for the wedding), but they are not sorry because they have become fed-up with having to listen to a non-stop eulogy about her man. Her work has, needless to say, also suffered from her inability to concentrate.

Malcolm is married and has a son who is 12 and a daughter of four. With his son he has what he describes as a 'brilliant relationship'. He cares deeply for his daughter, but he knows that his feelings for his son are far in excess of his love for both her and his wife. His job often takes him abroad, but he rings home every day. He always has long conversations with his son and sometimes even forgets to ask how anyone else in the family is getting on. When he brings presents home, the ones for his daughter are almost token in comparison with the extravagant purchases he has made for her brother. His wife is constantly getting angry with him about his unfair behaviour, of which he is often quite unaware. She has tried to be understanding because she knows that he is probably compensating for the poor relationship he had with his own father, and thinks it is quite reasonable that he should be closer to his son because they are both male and share so many interests. But she is now also feeling shut out by his obsessive love for his son, and losing patience with him even in front of the children. She has suggested that it might be best for them to separate. She knows she would get custody of both children, because her husband is away from home so much, and she is almost convinced that both children will benefit from seeing less of their father.

Not being unable to let go of relationships with people we love when they have left us and when it is in our own interests to start a 'new life':

Mick is 45 and divorced. His wife left him seven years ago for another man. During his time alone Mick has found himself only momentarily attracted to other women. He has tried several relationships, but as soon as they begin to get 'physical' Mick can only think of his former wife. He is not feeling particularly jealous of her new relationship – in fact, the two men have become close friends as Mick is always popping round to see them and babysits frequently for the children at their house. He always spends Christmas and other major events with them and is always there whenever they have any problems. He is often teased by his colleagues at work for his 'ménage à trois' lifestyle. To the outside world Mick doesn't appear pathetic or unhappy, but inwardly he knows he is still deeply in love with his ex-wife and feels very sad and lonely.

Gabrielle is 21. She spent most of the last two years of her school life nursing her widowed father through cancer. She did this willingly and efficiently and has no resentment about having had to put her own life on hold for a while. She is a bright girl who is quite capable of quickly recouping her educational losses. Her problem is more to do with the deep bond she established with her father during this period. Until he became too weak, they talked constantly – discussing books, his life, her life and the meaning of the universe in general. Now every other relationship in her life seems too superficial by comparison. She finds herself easily bored by both her male and female friends and her family. She is convinced that she will never marry because she knows no man could ever match up to her father. She still 'talks' to him each night before going to bed, and in her mind's eye consults him on every decision she makes. She doesn't appear to be in a state of grief – she says she cried her tears long before he died and feels that he is with her still anyway. But she doesn't think she would ever want leave his house, so chooses to work locally rather than go to university.

Spending too much of our time, emotional and physical energy and/or money on people, or one particular person we love, at the expense of our own welfare, self-esteem or other important relationships:

Karen is a 34-year-old woman who has had a successful career but now wants desperately to achieve the same kind of success in her personal life. She has had a series of relationships during the last 10 years but has noted that recently when a relationship is finished she is increasingly unable to let go. She finds herself not only obsessively thinking about her past boyfriend (to the detriment of her work) but also secretly following him around (to the detriment of her self-esteem).

Charles is a 55-year-old manager of his own engineering business which is still struggling to get back on its feet after the recession. He has been married very happily for the last 22 years and has three teenage children to whom he is devoted; he is also a much respected figure at work and in his local community. Two years ago, he employed a new young secretary, a school friend of his daughter's who was having difficulty finding a job. Much against his own 'better judgement', Charles found himself falling in love with this young woman. He is now leading a double life which is exhausting him physically and financially, but he feels totally at the mercy of his love for both his lover and his family. He knows what he is doing is wrong and is 'racked' by guilt which is eating away at his self-confidence. He also finds that he is needing more and more quick shots of whiskey to get him through the day.

ℚ Discussion ℚ

These few examples illustrate very poignantly how even love, the most revered of all our emotions, can wreak havoc with our lives if we allow it to get out of our control. None of these people is 'bad', in fact most would be admired for their above-average amounts of kindness, sensitivity and devotion to others.

These sad stories do not prove that we can have 'too much of a good thing' or we can be 'too' kind. They simply illustrate how an inability to control even an indisputably positive emotion such as love can undermine self-confidence and sabotage our chances of being happy and leading a successful life.

Can Unbridled Love Ever Be Good for Us?

Yes, of course it can, and it can be highly enjoyable as well! Some of the times when I have let my passion overwhelm me have been the most memorable of my life. I am not just talking about life in my bedroom, I am recalling other kinds of love as well! For example, there have been times when I allowed my love for my daughters or my compassion for my clients to overrule my head, and I have had no regrets about having had to mop up the consequences.

But although unbridled love, like riding bareback on a wild horse, can bring unforgettable joy and exhilaration and help stimulate our motivation to 'plod on' with our more mundane lives, I am sure you'd agree that it is a dangerously risky way to journey through our everyday relationships.

Why Do People Find It Hard to Be 'Sensible' about Love?

In the history of humanity, love has probably inspired more romantic myths than any other emotion. But in our modern society it is now undoubtedly idolized (e.g. 'It makes the world go round' and 'All you need is love'!). It is now considered vital, not just to happiness but to survival as well. People who aren't currently feeling it often think that their life is not worth living, and people who can't ever feel it are considered to be seriously sick and sometimes a danger to others. On the other hand, people who seem to feel it more deeply than most are often admired and envied in spite of the problems their 'passion' may bring them. The film stars Richard Burton and Liz Taylor will probably be remembered more for the depth of their love for each other than their respective acting skills. The myth of the Mafia enshrines them as much for their deep love for their families as their ruthless lives of crime.

So, if we find ourselves feeling this emotion with above-average intensity, it is hardly surprising that most people are reluctant to take any steps to control their feelings. Most would argue that it is beyond their power to do so anyway. It is commonly believed that love is an emotion with which we are 'blessed'. The degree to which we feel it, the time we feel it and for whom we feel it are all out of our control. It is often talked about as though it is an external force which descends upon us and leaves us without our consent (Cupid's arrow suddenly 'piercing our heart'; waking up one day to find our love has inexplicably 'gone cold').

These kinds of 'myths' in our brains about love make it hard for us sometimes to take responsibility for our own feelings and the actions we may take as a result of experiencing love, especially when it is felt profoundly. I know that when I was younger I actually took a kind of perverse pride in my ability to be 'swept off my feet', not just by lovers who were obviously no good for me, but also by clients who abused my compassion, and even by my children who manipulated me into giving in to their demands unwisely. Part of me thought I was a better person for feeling love in such a profound way that I would knowingly allow myself (and others) to be hurt by its effect on my behaviour. The historian Theodore Zeldin, who has written a fascinating account of the historical development of emotions, would probably say that I was seeking 'nobility' and escape from self-doubt. (And I'd have to agree he was 'spot on' with his diagnosis!) Fortunately I have now found additional routes to personal success and self-esteem, but I had many personal and several work disasters before I was motivated to look seriously at the way I managed this emotion.

Childhood Factors ✚

Factors in your childhood which may have programmed your brain with unhelpful and inappropriate unbridled love responses:

- Were you not loved enough by your parents?
- Did you lose someone whom you loved deeply? (especially if you were not well supported afterwards)
- Did you have a parent who couldn't control their love for either you or someone else?
- Did you have parents who didn't love each other, so that as a result your home life was cheerless and depressing?
- Was your own love and loving actions for your parents continually rejected? (e.g. 'Don't be soppy'; 'I've got too much to do, to sit down now' – or seeing your carefully crafted presents or laboriously drawn cards hidden away or binned)
- Did you have to earn love from your parents and other important figures by caring for them too often and at too young an age?

- Were you not supported and helped to cope when you first experimented with love relationships? (e.g. having our teenage all-consuming passions laughed at, or rejections dismissed as trivial)
- Were you fed with too many romantic tales about unbridled love in books, films or on TV?
- Did you have a life-script for 'unbridled love disasters' set in your mind, by being told continuously that you were too loving or too kind and that this would probably bring you trouble in later life (e.g. overhearing comments like 'Our Gloria is such a wonderful little girl, so loving, but she's going to get so hurt when she hits the real world')
- Were you a child in an unhappy family who used love as an escape? (e.g. either through fantasy, fuelled by magazines, etc., or through real-life romance)

Note down any other childhood experiences which may have had a significant influence on your ability to control your love.

Adult Habits 🗆

The following are common examples of adult habits which can keep unhelpful love responses active. They may be consciously or unconsciously practised. Do any sound familiar to you?

- depending too much on our love relationships to satisfy our need for self-esteem
- not healing efficiently from old love wounds, especially those from our childhood days
- putting the people we love on pedestals and refusing to look at or acknowledge their weaknesses
- feeding our need to be needed by keeping others unnecessarily dependent on us (e.g. doing too much for children instead of teaching them how to do things for themselves, or doing too much for a partner and not demanding that they do their 'fair share')
- keeping ourselves vulnerable to love by getting too lonely.

Tips for Better Management ☆

- Make it a habit to take time-out to think pragmatically and ask searching questions about all your key relationships (e.g. What are my expectations of each? Do I have any unwritten expectations or rules? Is there anything bugging me about this person? Is the other person leading the relationship too much?).
- Accustom yourself to solitude and firm up your independence by making your times alone reasonably frequent and highly enjoyable (e.g. go alone to restaurants and the cinema sometimes).

189

- Be routinely self-nurturing to yourself.
- Reward yourself after every achievement, and don't ever become dependent on the approval of the person you love to be able to enjoy your success.
- Don't always keep your innermost secrets for the ear of the person you love (either don't tell anyone or tell a few people).
- Watch out for neglecting your friendships when you start a 'special relationship' – be careful not to change your social life too radically.
- When you start making excuses for a loved one's behaviour, take extra care with that relationship.
- Be on your guard if the other person constantly wants to change you all the time and you start agreeing with them (at least outwardly).
- Always stand up assertively to put-downs from the people you love (sometimes that's harder to do than with someone who doesn't mean so much to us).
- Always take a breach of your own moral values very seriously (no relationship is worth damaging your self-respect for).
- After the break-up of a relationship, spend time with someone who can help you objectively to analyse what you can learn from the experience – don't just accept that love has 'miraculously' disappeared from either party's heart.
- From time to time, play devil's advocate to your love – force yourself to list some negative qualities about your loved one and a few problems you have with the relationship (if you cannot do this exercise, then it is time to seek help from someone who can!).

BALM ☐☐☐

Benefits

What do you stand to gain from taking more control over your unbridled love?:

I'll have more self-respect.

I'll have more respect from others.

I'll have better health.

What price could you ultimately pay for not taking more control of your unbridled love?:

I will destroy my relationship with ...

My career prospects will suffer.

My children could get hurt.

What treat are you going to give yourself for taking control of your unbridled love?:

A holiday in ...

A top-to-toe day at a health farm.

A year's subscription to a dating agency.

Attitudes

What inherited beliefs do you have programmed into your brain which are keeping you from taking more control over your unbridled love, and to whom do these really belong?:

'Take away love and our earth is a tomb' (Robert Browning and other poets who have idealized love out of all proportion!).

'Children always come first' (Mum).

'We only ever have one true love in life' (thousands of authors of novels and writers of film scripts).

What re-framed statements or affirmations could you use to counteract these beliefs?:

Even though love is important to me, there are many other ways of making my life worth living.

Putting myself first occasionally does not mean that I do not love my children enough.

I know many people who have found deep, intimate love with several people during their lives.

Which relevant quotes or sayings could you use to motivate and boost you?:

> *Love is one of the last refuges where a person can feel that he or she is able to achieve something noble, and receive the approval of another person: one of the few forms of success that can hold its own against self-doubt.*
>
> THEODORE ZELDIN

> *Love is like quicksilver in the hand. Leave the fingers open and it stays. Clutch it, and it darts away.*
>
> DOROTHY PARKER

> *The capacity to love demands a state of intensity, alertness, enhanced vitality, which can only be the result of a productive ... orientation in many other spheres of life. If one is not productive in other spheres, one is not productive in love.*
>
> ERICH FROMM

> *Love is a wonderful thing but as long as it is blind I will never be out of a job.*
>
> MR JUSTICE SELBY – DIVORCE COURT JUDGE

> *There are plenty more fish in the sea – I just need to keep up my swimming practice!*
>
> VARIATION ON A PROVERB BY GAEL!

What else will you do to help you take control of your unhelpful beliefs about love?:

Watch more comedy shows about relationships.

Write down on a small card a list of six things other than love that make my life worth living and use this card as a bookmark for the next few months.

Lifestyle

What changes in your lifestyle will you make to ensure that you remain more in control of your unbridled love?:

Keep Tuesday and Thursday nights for *me*.

Set aside one evening a month just for our relationship, and make sure we have an honest talk about how things are going on between us (and not about what needs doing to the flat, or work or ...).

Join a parenting class.

Management

What are your chief warning signs that your love is becoming unbridled?:

I start worrying unnecessarily about where she is and if she is safe.

I stop going out with my friends.

I've missed three important matches in a row.

I start excusing his insensitive behaviour.

I lose/gain weight.

Which strategies can you use to help you take more control of your love?:

Assertiveness (*see pages 44, 76*).

Affirmations (*see page 38*).

What is your step-by-step action plan?:

On Tuesday I will ask ... for a date when we can talk.

By the end of the month I will have an appointment with a relationship counsellor and/or start to read a book on relationship skills.

By the end of the year I will be in a new relationship.

Whom will you ask to support you while you are working on your unbridled love habits?:

_____.

_____.

_____.

2

Maintaining
Emotional Confidence

I do hope you have found this programme interesting and, even more importantly, useful. For some of you, this approach to managing your feelings may have been a radically new one. For others it could have been just a helpful reminder of old wisdom which perhaps in the heat of emotion you sometimes forget. Much of what I have written about I have known for many years, but I have found that writing it down has been very useful and has certainly given my own emotional confidence an encouraging boost.

It is highly likely that I shall be giving many talks and workshops on this subject during the next few years. I shall therefore, without any *extra* effort, be lucky enough to have my learning constantly reinforced. But, unless you too are in my line of business, you may need to take more care to ensure that you don't forget what you have learned. One of the ways you can do this is by **keeping this book in a handy place for the next few months** and dipping into it from time to time.

Another very important way is to use your knowledge and skill to **help others build their emotional confidence**. I am not suggesting that you start lecturing and confronting people with what *you* think they are feeling, or pass judgements on how they ought to be feeling or acting. (This would certainly be a quick route to losing friends and alienating colleagues!) But you could, for example, try to:

– use your knowledge and skill to respond more sensitively and less judgementally to others' emotional mistakes
– share your own experiences and knowledge in an unthreatening way (e.g. say what has helped you, but add that you realize it may not necessarily be what would help them)

or,

– you could just remind yourself that your most effective helping tool will always be your own example! I hope you will agree that this is yet another compelling reason to inspire you to keep your own emotional confidence in sturdy shape!

Finally, here are three handy rules to help keep you on track!

Emotional Confidence Maintenance Rules!

1. Regularly practise the key techniques for harnessing 'automatic' responses.
2. Repair emotional hurts quickly and thoroughly.
3. Look for and enjoy the positive potential in every emotion.

Further Reading
and Resources

Books

Summaries of Research on Emotion

Paul Ekman and Richard J. Davidson, *The Nature of Emotion* (OUP, 1994)

Daniel Goleman, *Emotional Intelligence* (Bantam, 1995)

Rom Harre and W. Gerrod Parrott, *The Emotions: Social, Cultural and Biological Dimensions* (Sage, 1996)

Richard S. Lazarus, *Emotion and Adaptation* (OUP, 1991)

Theodore Zeldin, *An Intimate History of Humanity* (Minerva, 1994)

Sources of Quotations

Eileen Campbell, *A Dancing Star: Inspirations to Guide and Heal* (Thorsons, 1992)

John-Roger and Peter McWilliams, *You Can't Afford the Luxury of a Negative Thought* (Thorsons, 1990)

Useful Techniques

Carla Hannaford, *Smart Moves* (Arlington, VA: Great Ocean
    Publishers, 1995)
Robert Holden, *Stress Busters* (Thorsons, 1992)
Gael Lindenfield, *Assert Yourself* (Thorsons, 1986)
—, *The Positive Woman* (Thorsons, 1992)
—, *Self-esteem* (Thorsons, 1995)
Ronald Shone, *Creative Visualization* (Thorsons, 1984)
Paul Wilson, *Instant Calm* (Penguin, 1995)

Handling and Understanding Specific Feelings

Jonathan Bradshaw, *Healing the Shame that Binds You* (Florida,
    US: Health Communications Inc., 1988)
Nancy Friday, *Jealousy* (Fontana, 1989)
Erich Fromm, *The Art of Loving* (Mandala, 1975)
Dr Kenneth Hambly, *Banish Anxiety* (Thorsons, 1991)
Judith Lewis Herman, *Trauma and Recovery* (Pandora, 1992)
Susan Jeffers, *Feel the Fear and Do it Anyway* (Arrow, 1987)
Gael Lindenfield, *Managing Anger* (Thorsons, 1993)
Susie Orbach and Luise Eichenbaum, *Bittersweet: Love, envy
    and competition in women's friendships* (Arrow, 1987)
Dorothy Rowe, *Beyond Fear* (Fontana, 1987)

Cassettes

Daniel Goleman, *Emotional Intelligence* (Thorsons Audio, 1997)
Gael Lindenfield, *Emotional Confidence* (Thorsons Audio, 1997)
A wide range of relaxation cassettes are available in most
    bookshops.

Games

A range of games for personal and professional use, as well as books and cassettes designed to help people develop better emotional health, are available by mail order from:

Being Yourself
Tel: 01304 226 900
Fax: 01304 226 700

Courses and Seminars
Led by Gael Lindenfield

Please contact the publicity department of Thorsons (address at the front of this book) for information on Gael Lindenfield's consultancy.

Index